MASSIVE OPEN ONLINE COURSES

Are MOOCs a catalyst for reimagining education, a sign of the increased corporatization of the education sector, or merely a well-publicized but passing trend? *Massive Open Online Courses* shares insights from multiple stakeholders on what MOOCs are now and could eventually become, providing those in higher education as well as K–12, military, government, and corporate training with an authoritative source on a wide range of key issues surrounding MOOCs.

MOOCs, or Massive Open Online Courses, are a disruptive technology currently forcing a serious reconceptualization of accreditation, assessment, motivation and retention, technology-based instruction, and the overall student experience. In this timely volume, Paul Kim brings together experts from higher education, business, law, learning analytics and other relevant areas to provide an evenhanded, research-based positioning of MOOCs within the existing educational technology landscape and a base for understanding whether they could reshape the future of education.

Paul Kim is the Chief Technology Officer and Assistant Dean of the Graduate School of Education at Stanford University. Dr. Kim serves on the Board of Directors of WestEd, the Committee on Grand Challenges in International Development for the National Academies of Science, and the advisory committee for the National Science Foundation's Education and Human Resources Directorate.

MASSIVE OPEN ONLINE COURSES

The MOOC Revolution

Edited by Paul Kim

Routledge
Taylor & Francis Group

NEW YORK AND LONDON

First published 2015
by Routledge
711 Third Avenue, New York, NY 10017

and by Routledge
2 Park Square, Milton Park, Abingdon, Oxon OX14 4RN

Routledge is an imprint of the Taylor & Francis Group, an informa business

© 2015 Taylor & Francis

The right of Paul Kim to be identified as the author of the editorial material of this work, and of the authors for their individual chapters, has been asserted by them in accordance with sections 77 and 78 of the Copyright, Designs and Patents Act 1988.

Trademark notice: Product or corporate names may be trademarks or registered trademarks, and are used only for identification and explanation without intent to infringe.

Library of Congress Cataloging-in-Publication Data
Massive open online courses: the MOOC revolution/edited by
  Paul Kim.
  pages cm
  Includes bibliographical references and index.
  1. MOOCs (Web-based instruction) 2. Distance education.
  3. Educational technology. I. Kim, Paul (Hongsuk)
  LB1044.87.M275 2014
  371.33'44678—dc23
  2014022493

ISBN: 978-0-415-73308-3 (hbk)
ISBN: 978-0-415-73309-0 (pbk)
ISBN: 978-1-315-84865-5 (ebk)

Typeset in Bembo and Stone Sans
by Florence Production Ltd, Stoodleigh, Devon, UK

Printed and bound in the United States of America by
Edwards Brothers Malloy on sustainably sourced paper

CONTENTS

Introduction   vii
Paul Kim

1   The Anatomy of MOOCs   1
Jane E. Klobas, Bruce Mackintosh, and Jamie Murphy

2   MOOC Pedagogy   23
Sian Bayne and Jen Ross

3   To MOOC or Not to MOOC? University Decision-
Making and Agile Governance for Educational Innovation   46
Jeff Haywood and Hamish Macleod

4   Enter the Anti-MOOCs: The Reinvention of Online
Learning as a Form of Social Commentary   61
Larry Johnson and Samantha Adams Becker

5   Developing a Sustainable MOOC Business Model   78
Victor Hu

6   The Subject Matters: MOOCs and Relevancy   90
Dennis Yang and Meg Evans

7   NovoEd, a Social Learning Environment   96
Farnaz Ronaghi, Amin Saberi, and Anne Trumbore

8   MOOCs, Copyright, and the Many Meanings of "Open"   106
    Samantha Bernstein

9   Educating Educators: Designing MOOCs for Professional
    Learning   117
    Glenn M. Kleiman, Mary Ann Wolf, and David Frye

    Contributing Authors   147
    Index   153

INTRODUCTION

Paul Kim

The emergence of Massively Open Online Courses (MOOCs) has been a fast-growing trend over the past few years, receiving both high acclaim and criticism with respect to how it will change the education landscape. As many areas of society have undergone rapid changes enabled by technology, the education sector has been by comparison in a dormant state for some time. Thus, it was inevitable that technology enthusiasts and experimenters would create something like MOOCs and use technology to open up new educational possibilities. Even though MOOCs may not live up to all of the initial hype that accompanied them, and we are still trying to figure out the best way to use them, there is no doubt that they are an important new innovation with the potential to have a large impact. For this reason, I thought it would be a good time to edit a book about MOOCs that covers various aspects of the MOOC phenomenon that are not discussed in depth.

The key point to keep in mind when thinking about MOOCs (or any educational technology interventions, for that matter) is that the primary focus should not be the technology, but rather the pedagogy (more strictly, androgogy in the higher education context, but we can stick with the more broadly used term, "pedagogy"). Although technology may enable or prevent certain pedagogical elements, it would be thinking backwards to value only what is possible and to ignore what is infeasible. Thus, we should start by trying to focus on the learning experiences we want to create, and then trying to enable that with technology. We do want to keep in mind, of course, that technical possibilities often inspire new ideas for pedagogy, so there is a reciprocal relationship. Up to this point in the short history of MOOCs, technology has been overemphasized at the expense of pedagogy. **Jane E. Klobas**, **Bruce Mackintosh**, and **Jamie Murphy** introduce us to the landscape of MOOCs, including a breakdown of the acronym, its roots in the open education movement, and describe each of the main groups in the MOOC ecosystem: the providers, platforms, pedagogy, and the users.

It is clear when considered as an ecosystem that MOOCs represent significant innovations, particularly in their distribution models, which dramatically lower entry barriers (free tuition, open or freely licensed resources, etc.), and also in their delivery models, which enable dramatically lower teacher-to-student ratios (e.g. via recorded lectures, auto-graded assignments, peer reviews, lightly monitored discussion forums, etc.). However, besides the distribution and delivery models, those developing MOOCs should focus on learning models, which focus on how students will actually learn in the course. Although some may assume that the MOOC platform being used largely dictates the pedagogical approach, **Sian Bayne** and **Jen Ross**, in our book edition, state that pedagogy is not embedded in the MOOC platforms, and walk through three case studies to show how pedagogy emerges from various facets of the course—something that is not captured by the binary attribution of an "xMOOC" versus a "cMOOC."

While designing the pedagogy is the primary focus for a teacher designing a course, when considering innovations in education, we need to take into account the larger ecosystem that the teaching and learning take place in. We need to take into account the goals, motivations, and experiences of learners, teachers, institutions, and other third-parties. **Jeff Haywood** and **Hamish Macleod** discuss the university point of view in terms of motivation (reputation, R&D, future opportunities, etc.), coordination (top-down university-led vs. bottom-up faculty-led), and decisions (platform selection, course selection, and frequency), with more specific insight into the University of Edinburgh's approach. **Victor Hu** discusses the MOOC platform providers, and the primary challenge that they are facing, that of determining a sustainable business model—he discusses a variety of potential tactics, including ones that are most prevalent today (verified certificates of completion), and those that seem promising (licensing of educational content to other institutions). It is clear that given their important enabling role, it is in everyone's interests for the MOOC platform providers to become sustainable. The insertion of the MOOC platform providers as another party in the teacher–university relationship also raises additional (and opens up old) legal issues. **Samantha Bernstein** describes some of the legal challenges related to the status of copyrights for faculty-generated content, student work, and third-party materials. With MOOCs allowing a much larger scale for materials to be disseminated, content rights, fair use, and licensing will all need new conversations. Each of the players in the ecosystem described here face individual challenges, but an additional challenge to driving change is to get all of them to be in synch, since each operates at separate "clockspeeds." Unless there is a major crisis (though some might reasonably argue that there is), change will likely happen in fits and starts, and will resemble evolution rather than a major disruption.

Even as we consider the educational ecosystem for MOOCs as they currently are, we are also seeing further experiments in the evolution and adaptation of MOOCs themselves. **Larry Johnson** and **Samantha Adams Becker** discuss what have been termed "anti-MOOCs," efforts possibly driven by disenchantment and criticism from the low rates of engagement in the traditional, large, popular MOOCs. Johnson and Becker give examples of various "anti-MOOCs," which are all adaptations of MOOCs to apply to smaller student groups, often at a single university. However, the fact that these efforts still retain many elements of traditional MOOCs shows that, despite their shortcomings, many of the elements behind MOOCs do provide strong educational value. Also, these efforts will hopefully shed more light on pedagogical factors that will enhance the design or inform the suitability of the larger MOOCs. Another example of adapting MOOCs are platforms that follow many MOOC design principles but may charge for some or all of its courses. An example is Udemy, where **Dennis Yang** and **Meg Evans** make the case that a marketplace model can be an appropriate way to signal educational content that is in demand (versus the typical current practice of professors choosing content) and also attracts other experts (not sponsored by an educational institution) to provide content. Another MOOC platform provider, NovoEd, as described by **Farnaz Ronaghi**, **Amin Saberi**, and **Anne Trumbore**, acknowledges that learning is a social act, and has explicitly designed its platform to try to move beyond the lecture hall model paradigm in a way that is scalable. They describe the design principles they have incorporated into the platform to facilitate collaboration and project-based learning, through mechanisms such as participant reputational ranking, algorithmic team formation, and non-anonymous peer reviews. Given the great diversity of learning needs across the globe, a large portion of which is already met by paid educational experiences, it seems that there can be an important role for paid MOOC platforms and providers as well.

Up to this point we have covered pedagogy for the learner, universities, platform providers, and alternate adaptations of the traditional MOOCs. It is now time to talk more about the teacher's role with respect to MOOCs. Criticisms of "xMOOCs," which incorporate transplanted lecture-based methods to a new medium, are in many cases criticisms directed at teachers who choose to follow these methods. However, it is important to note that teaching is not a discipline easily characterized by innovation, so it is difficult to change. Even with the early adopter cohort of adventurous professors who have been developing MOOCs thus far, it is often a challenge just to record straightforward video lectures— teachers too will need time to change. As discussed earlier, they have the burden of designing the pedagogy of the course, as well as executing it. Thus, with the critical role they play they need help, and it can be offered in several ways. Teachers sponsored by universities should receive compensation or course relief for their MOOC teaching activities. Also, the expertise of an educational technologist is required: someone who keeps up with best practices with respect to technology to show the teaching team what is feasible, but who also understands learning theory and can help provide guidance to the teacher in designing effective pedagogy to reach the educational aims of the course. In some situations, this expertise may reside in two individuals, and in other cases, the teacher himself or herself might be an expert in one of the roles. In many cases, perhaps, the expertise cannot be found or cannot be budgeted, and the teacher will need to make do the best they can. However, when universities and teachers are planning to develop MOOCs, they should understand what is really required to develop effective ones. Fittingly, there are efforts to train teachers at a substantial scale via MOOCs, and one example is **Glenn Kleiman**, **Mary Ann Wolf**, and **David Frye**, who describe their MOOC-Ed initiative to provide professional development for K-12 teachers, resulting in strong positive feedback after the two initial courses. Though the MOOC-Ed series of MOOCs are primarily focused on K-12 teachers, it is hoped that they will develop insights into training educators more generally, and this can be applied to training the next cohorts of teachers to develop the MOOCs in the future.

In 2012, I developed and delivered a MOOC titled *Designing a New Learning Environment* (DNLE), which reached over 18,000 students in 170 countries. Although I did not get to meet most of them in person, I learned a great deal from the experiences and voices of the students as they engaged with the course and collaborated with each other. The DNLE has turned into a Massive Ongoing Online Collaboration. One participant, Charlie Chung, eventually later provided editorial assistance on this book! I would like to thank those students for their continuous inspiration.

I hope you enjoy this book and the perspectives the authors bring from different areas of the MOOC space. Please do not hesitate to contact any of us with any questions, ideas, or comments that you may have. Together, let's design a new learning environment!

1

THE ANATOMY OF MOOCS

Jane E. Klobas, Bruce Mackintosh, and Jamie Murphy

Introduction

MOOCs are more than just massive, open, online courses. The notion of the MOOC is coupled with: the strengths and limitations of the information technology platforms that make them possible; the relative merits of the providers of both platforms and courses (edX, Coursera, and others); and the value of the very idea that courses can be offered by the best teachers from the best universities, at no charge, to anyone who wishes to enroll. This chapter peels MOOCs back to their fundamentals, uncovering the anatomy of MOOC courses, platforms, and multiple levels of provider and user in the evolving MOOC market. It presents MOOCs as an educational innovation that combines and extends the capabilities of existing technologies, and draws on a range of approaches to e-learning to offer a new educational product in a new way to new markets.

We begin by dissecting the M, O, O, and C in MOOC, then flesh MOOCs out by examining them from four perspectives (as illustrated in Figure 1.1). We first consider the technical MOOC platform, which both enables and constrains what can be done in a course run as a MOOC. We then focus on MOOCs as courses, examining current practices in relation to educational theory, before sharing observations about the complexity of the provider side of the MOOC market. Finally, we consider questions about use and user acceptance of MOOCs, before closing with some conclusions about what the current status of MOOCs implies for the evolution of education and training.

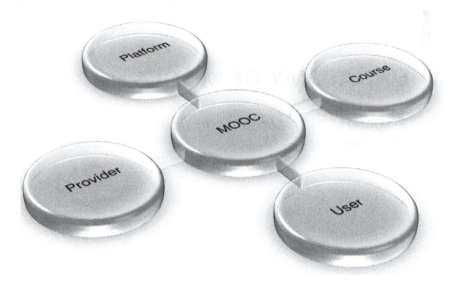

FIGURE 1.1 Four perspectives on MOOCs

MOOC: Breaking Down the Acronym

The fundamental, defining aspects of MOOCs are outlined in Figure 1.2. MOOCs are courses offered online at a distance, and open—at no charge—to any participant who wishes to enroll. The underlying technology has the capacity to accommodate many thousands (a "massive" number) of participants. We consider each of these aspects of MOOCs in more detail in this section.

M	**Massive** capacity
O	**Open** to all: participants have diverse abilities and backgrounds; no fees are charged for participation
O	**Online,** at a distance
C	**Course**: a systematic sequence of learning activities

FIGURE 1.2 The defining characteristics of MOOCs

- M for Massive refers to the capacity of MOOCs to accommodate very large numbers of learners, well beyond the numbers that can be accommodated in classrooms or that had participated in online courses prior to the first MOOC. There is no specific number associated with "massive." When the term MOOC was first coined, it referred to a course of 2,200 students (Cormier, 2008; Downes, 2009). Several MOOCs have since attracted more than 150,000 registrations (Jordan, 2014).

The capacity of MOOCs to be massive reflects developments in information and communications technology (ICT) and the pedagogy of online and distance learning, as illustrated in Figure 1.3. Relevant ICT advances[1] include:

- infrastructure and software services to store, index and remotely access very large amounts of digital content (e.g., YouTube, Google Books, digital libraries, cloud computing archives);
- secure registration and identification of very large numbers of users (needed for social media); and
- robust, reliable, and secure software and services for simultaneous access by very large numbers of users to the same Web pages and media (as occurs with social media).

MOOCs also bring together advances in online and distance learning from several branches of pedagogy and educational technology, including Web-enhanced learning, connectivism,[2] learning management systems (LMS), e-learning, computer-supported collaborative learning (CSCL), open and distance learning, and computer-based education and training (CBT). The need to reach and serve a massive number of learners has consolidated these developments, and resulted in further innovation.

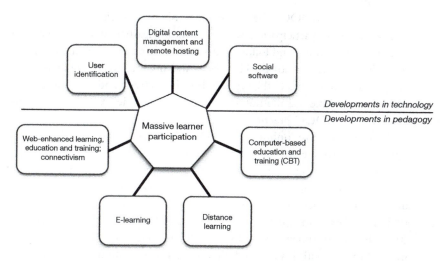

FIGURE 1.3 Some developments that enable MOOCs to be massive

New technical issues associated with the large scale of MOOCs are being resolved as they arise (Hunt & Mares, 2013; Martin & Gil, 2013), so MOOC technology appears to be scalable to meet demand. The technical capacity for massive enrolments, combined with an openness to acceptance of all learners who register for a MOOC (see O for Open, below) also has significant implications for MOOC pedagogy, which we discuss in a separate section.

- O for Open has several different interpretations in the MOOC arena. The most common are outlined in Table 1.1.

Two other types of openness appear to be emerging along with MOOCs, according to a White Paper prepared by the UK Centre for Educational Technology, Interoperability and Standards (CETIS). These are *open assessment*, in which the learner chooses whether or not to have their work assessed, replacing the existing institutional monopoly on formal assessment with "on-demand accreditation," and *open curriculum*, in which the learner creates their own curriculum by selecting courses from those available (Yuan & Powell, 2013).

- O for Online defines MOOCs as online courses, regardless of their relationship to classroom-based courses and activities. The first course to be described as a MOOC, Connectivism and Connective Knowledge (CCK08), was an online open learning course offered (at a distance) in 2008 by George Siemens and Stephen Downes at the University of Manitoba in Canada. Of the 2,200 participants, only 24 were enrolled for university credit (Downes, 2009). Many MOOCs still have a classroom analog. Some, but not all, of these courses are offered simultaneously to both enrolled and non-enrolled participants.

Whether the MOOC is held simultaneously with its classroom analog or not, most online participation is asynchronous: learners choose their own time to access content and follow course activities rather than attend online, "live" lectures and meetings. The places and times at which segments of a MOOC are offered affect the types of learning activity and technology that can be used. Table 1.2 illustrates a range of possibilities, with observations from current MOOC practice.

Because they are online and open, MOOCs can be used as open educational resources (OERs) for classroom-based courses. A MOOC can be embedded in a traditional classroom-based course to transform it into a blended learning course; part of the learning takes place online, in the MOOC, and part face-to-face in the classroom. A specific adaptation of this model is a "flipped classroom" (Baker, 2000; Fisher, 2012; Forsey, Low, & Glance, 2013), in which students study by MOOC at home and classroom sessions are used to deal with issues and difficulties that arise from the "homework." Regardless of the approach used, the MOOC itself remains online.

TABLE 1.1 Some definitions of "open" in the MOOCs arena, and their use

Definition	Explanation	Use
Open access	a. Open to all. No restriction on age, prior learning or qualification, or other source of individual, physical, or intellectual difference. b. No charge is made for any aspect of the course or acknowledgement of completion.	a. Generally accepted. Even courses that suggest that students have some prior learning do not check for prior learning. b. The most common approach, although acknowledgement of completion, is not offered for all courses. Acknowledgements issued at no cost are usually in the form of a digital badge or certificate. Acknowledgements issued by course aggregators may include a grade or course rank. Graded certificates are available at payment for some courses. Teacher and university of origin are usually named.
Open education	Application of policies and practices to increase access to formal education for learners who face physical, cognitive, geographical, temporal or other barriers to participation, implemented by open universities and other open educational institutions.[1]	Although MOOC descriptions usually refer only to overcoming geographical and temporal barriers, open universities in the UK (The Open University), Spain (UNED: Universidad Nacional de Educación a Distancia) and Australia (Open Universities Australia) are taking key roles in MOOC development.
Philosophically "open"	Adopts principals of openness in rights for reproduction and reuse of material and access to the source code for information systems; follows open standards for software development. Openness of this kind can be seen in use of open standards and formats for coding, storing, and sharing learning resources and data. Openly available learning resources are known as open educational resources (OERs) (OECD Centre for Educational Research and Innovation, 2007).	A MOOC can be used as an OER, and embedded within other courses. Open standards and formats, such as the Sharable Content Object Reference Model (SCORM) for course content and Dublin Core metadata for web resources, are rarely discussed in relation to MOOCs. Detail about openness in MOOC technology is provided in the section on MOOC platforms.
Open scheduling	Learners may take the course at any time, on any dates, and over any period they select.	Udacity,[2] and training providers, often offer courses this way. Open scheduling is less common for courses offered by universities.

Continued . . .

TABLE 1.1 *Continued*

Notes

1 Open education, or open learning, differs from open pedagogy. Open pedagogy is an approach to learning based on Illich's (1971) proposal to replace institutionalized learning with "educational webs" in which technology supports exchanges of knowledge through learning networks. It is only seen in connectivist MOOCs (cMOOCs).

2 Udacity, one of the first MOOC aggregators, has changed its business model to become an online course provider. Udacity now charges a subscription for course participation (material download is free) and caps course enrolments: www.udacity.com

TABLE 1.2 Possible variations in learning activities and technologies, by place and time of MOOC participation

Place	Time	
	Same time *(Synchronous)*	**Different time** *(Asynchronous)*
	Face-to-Face (FTF) Learning	***Continuous Group Activities***
Same Place *(Colocated)*	Activities might include lectures, individual learning activities, and group learning activities.	Group learning activities that involve sharing knowledge and resources in a physical location, even if the participants are not there at the same time.
	Technology: In a classroom or other physical learning space, enhanced with digital capture, display, projection, and interaction tools, connected to the Internet.	*Technology*: In a team room or other allocated physical learning space, enhanced with tools to support asynchronous completion of group learning activities, e.g., wall display, project management board, decision support system, groupware, content management system.
	Synchronous Online Interaction	***Asynchronous Online Distance Learning***
Different Place *(Online distance learning, ODL)*	*Activities*: Several practical limitations hinder remote synchronous activities, including the difficulty of adequately capturing a full audio record of interactions (although audio capture of an instructor is straightforward) and insufficient bandwidth in many locations. MOOCs deal with this issue by limiting synchronous interaction.	*Activities*: Many MOOCs are designed specifically as asynchronous ODL courses. Activities vary considerably, depending on the pedagogical focus and training of the educators and the capabilities of the technology used.

Continued . . .

TABLE 1.2 *Continued*

Technology: Opportunities to use real-time online broadcast lectures, online virtual worlds such as Second Life, and even voice over IP such as Skype are limited. With few exceptions (primarily with relatively small student cohorts), synchronicity in MOOCs is limited to instant messaging or voice over IP calls between students, with some live chat.	*Technology*[1]: xMOOCs emphasize tools to a) capture knowledge (e.g., short lectures and instructor-created exercises) and package it for delivery to students, and b) test students on that knowledge. Bulletin boards and discussion forums are used rarely and relatively small subsets of learners self-organize on social media. Incorporation of regular teacher forum participation and Twitter feeds into xMOOCs do not appear to produce adequate return on effort (Parr, 2013). cMOOCs make more use of social and knowledge sharing tools, including wikis.

Note

1 See C for Course, below, for distinction between cMOOCs and xMOOCs.

- C for Course reminds us that the foundation of MOOCs, whether considered in terms of the merits of different providers and platforms, strategies, or business models, is still a course, i.e., a systematic sequence of learning activities. Courses need to be designed, developed, run, evaluated, and revised, and the effort involved in these tasks is considerable—particularly when they are open to massive numbers of learners of diverse abilities and backgrounds, and offered online. A distinction is made between cMOOCs (connectivist MOOCs[3]), and MOOCs that adopt a different pedagogy, particularly the content delivery style synonymous with courses offered by large aggregators such as Coursera and edX, known as "xMOOCs" (Siemens, 2012). Mounting a MOOC can involve substantial cost and a large and highly skilled team (Edinburgh University MOOC Teams, 2013; Head, 2013; Parr, 2013).

The MOOC Platform

The term "MOOC platform" is used almost exclusively to describe xMOOC software environments that assist MOOC designers, developers, and course writers to build courses, instructors to deliver courses, and students to participate in courses. We concentrate on xMOOC environments in the first part of this section. cMOOCs incorporate a wide variety of software in a network of connections that is unique to each course, as we discuss at the end of this section.

In its simplest sense, a MOOC platform is the software that runs the MOOC. The software sits on hardware, and enables interactions with the Internet and the servers that store course materials and information about learners and their progress.

Both proprietary and open source MOOC platforms exist. The most well-known proprietary platforms are those developed by the MOOC providers, Coursera and Udacity. Open source MOOC platforms include Google's Course Builder, which is being incorporated into Open edX, and OpenMOOC, supported by UNED (*Universidad Nacional de Educación a Distancia*), a Spanish university with long experience in open distance learning, and the CSEV (Centro Superior para la Enseñanza Virtual) foundation for online education, also in Spain.

MOOC platforms typically offer:

- identity access management (IAM) or seamless interface to institutional IAM systems, for management of MOOC access;
- a content management system or a set of services that identify and manage or point to learning resources in different locations and different formats;
- a quiz generator or seamless interface to a set of quiz and learning activity generators;
- a bulletin board service, blog, or seamless interface to an external blogging service;
- a discussion forum or seamless interface to an environment that permits discussion or questions and answers;
- a wiki or seamless interface to an external wiki (less common than bulletin boards and forums);
- services that provide links to the World Wide Web and the wider Internet;
- a course development environment or a seamless interface to such an environment;
- the teacher interface to the course;
- the learner interface to the course;
- services that identify and deliver learning resources and utilities to the learner when required;
- administrative tools for reporting and enabling "learning analytics" (detailed analysis of data concerning user access and progress while using the platform).

Table 1.3 lists some xMOOC platform tools by the online learning system or resource in which MOOC users might first have encountered them.

MOOC learning resources are generally developed or sourced from outside the MOOC platform. A variety of audio and video recording and editing, lecture capture, and other multimedia tools is used to produce the media.

Open source initiatives touch on MOOC platforms in several ways. In addition to open source MOOC platforms, open source content management and e-learning systems are being used to build MOOC platforms. A robust example

TABLE 1.3 Examples of xMOOC platform tools encountered in other online learning systems

Tools available in xMOOC platforms include	Previously developed for or commonly seen in
Content upload	Learning Management Systems (LMS)
Bulletin boards	LMS
Discussion forums	LMS
Atomic content (learning resources produced and presented in small chunks, e.g., short video lectures)	E-learning development tools
Screen capture for illustration of methods, techniques	E-learning development tools
Use of open educational resources (OERs)	Connection to the wider Internet
YouTube as a source of OERs	Connection to social media
Quizzes and tests with immediate student feedback and adaptive learning[1]	Computer-based training
Twitter and Facebook as media for student interaction	Connection to social media

Note

1 Adaptive learning is yet to be employed widely in MOOCs.

is the Open2Study platform (Open Universities Australia), which is based on open source systems—the Drupal content management system, and the Moodle e-learning and learning management system—and uses Amazon's hosting services and tools (Hunt & Mares, 2013).

Most MOOC platform interfaces are available only in English and little has been done specifically to address access by learners with physical or cognitive impairment. Open source initiatives are addressing language issues, e.g. Miriada X is a fully Spanish and Portuguese MOOC based on OpenMOOC. Several initiatives exist in China to translate or subtitle Coursera courses, but at the time of writing, not the platform itself (Lee, 2013).

cMOOCs do not have a specific platform, although they have a home page and course design that defines learning activities and, typically, space for aggregating ideas, questions, and knowledge connections. The detailed list provided by Downes (2009) for CCK08 provides an idea of the variety of software that can support a cMOOC. Connectivist learning is open to new resources, including software resources and student-created resources, as the stylized network map in Figure 1.4 shows.

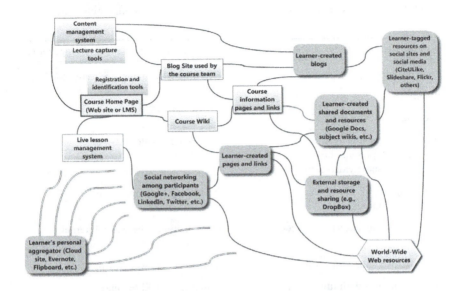

FIGURE 1.4 Network of software, media and content connections in a hypothetical cMOOC (inspired by Melcher, 2008). Detail of connections with Content management system and Learner's personal aggregator is omitted

The MOOC as a Course

The massive, open, and online nature of MOOCs both challenges and constrains course designers. MOOCs are online courses, mediated by information and communications technology. The types of learning material and activity included in a course are limited by the technology's capabilities and "affordances" (the actions that educators perceive they can take using the technology (Gibbons, 1986)). The teacher interface to an xMOOC platform establishes the affordances of the platform, regardless of what the platform developer intended. Openness to any learner, anywhere, at almost any time, requires careful consideration of achievable learning objectives, appropriate sequence and pace, and satisfactory methods, among other aspects of course design. The very large number of learners participating in the course offers challenges in terms of interaction and assessment.

Among the pedagogical decisions that a MOOC course designer and teacher must make are:

- Purpose and audience:
  - The goal of the course.
  - Learning objectives.
  - Level of the course (taking into account the open nature of enrolments).

- Course timing, pacing and effort:

  - Start and end dates, e.g., open, or fixed (typically to or within a university or college semester, or fixed according to teacher availability).
  - Course length. Current MOOCs range from 2–3 weeks to 15–26 weeks long, with training and personal development courses typically shorter, and university courses typically five weeks or longer.
  - Pace. Options include: entirely student self-paced, set weekly activities with or without fixed deadlines, and a combination of these options. Most courses offered by universities involve weekly activities or deadlines, particularly if the course can be taken for assessment.
  - Student effort expected. The number of hours of student effort to be committed in each period or for each activity needs to be estimated. This is important for student preparation and planning, and also for accreditation of MOOCs where credits and credit transfers are granted.

- Course structure. Because each learning component needs to be pre-designed and, usually, pre-packaged, objectives-based design tends to be used more than topic-based design. Each session is thus defined by what the participants are to learn, and content and learning activities are directed toward the specific learning objectives for the session. Quizzes and assessments also address the learning objectives.

- Course content:

  - Multimedia. xMOOC content is typically based on short videos (5–10 minutes). Videos that include a combination of tablet drawing, slides, and the lecturer's "talking head" are engaging (Guo, Kim, & Rubin, 2014).
  - Intellectual property (IP). Ensure rights are available, or obtained, for material developed by others; decide on IP and rights protection for new material.
  - Design exercises and other active learning activities (e.g., reflections on content presented or read so far, independent Web searches on specific topics, math, and coding tasks).
  - Quizzes and self-assessment. To what extent will they be integrated with videos or separate from them?
  - Sequencing. Linear, or will learners be permitted to branch to different content, or make their own connections, throughout the course, or at different stages? Most xMOOCs currently offer only linear sequencing.

- Designed interaction. Effective interaction in forums and discussions requires design of questions and structure rather than a laissez-faire approach.
- Assessment. What will be assessed and when? Will learners be permitted to re-take an assessment? What combination of computer-based assessment, self-assessment, and peer assessment will be used? Will assessment standards be

moderated externally? Will verified identification of learners be required for accreditation, and will verification be entirely online or require physical presence at a testing center?

The full course outlines provided by Open2Study (www.open2study.com/) illustrate how this detail can be brought together and presented to learners. Full detail of the Connectivism and Connective Knowledge course run by Downes and Siemens in 2011, including detail of the content and media used, is available at http://cck11.mooc.ca/.

MOOC Providers

There are several overlapping types of MOOC provider. Table 1.4 differentiates between them by function, leaving it to Chapter 6 to consider MOOC business models.

Working with this group of providers are course designers, the authors of OERs, learning analysts, and others who are essential to the operation of MOOCs.

Adoption and Acceptance of MOOCs

The variety of roles involved in MOOC provision alone suggests that MOOC adoption and acceptance is complicated. As illustrated in Figure 1.5, aggregators, hubs, and platform providers operate in a kind of two-sided market (Eisenmann, Parker, & Van Alstyne, 2006), where survival depends on *course providers* on the one hand, and on *MOOC users* on the other.

Institutional Course Providers

Institutional course providers include universities, teaching colleges, and training organizations: the number exceeds 350,[4] and is growing. The majority are elite US universities (Haggard & others, 2013), although there has also been strong uptake in the UK and Spain, both of which have a long tradition of open universities. Universities in Canada, Australia, New Zealand, China, India, Africa, Germany, and elsewhere in mainland Europe have also adopted MOOCs.

The main reasons that university administrators give for adopting MOOCs combine learning about massive online education and using MOOCs to build reputation and showcase star faculty (Grajek, Bischel, & Dahlstrom, 2013; The Chronicle of Higher Education, 2013). Some institutions hope to obtain a financial return or reduce costs, and others are committed to making their courses openly accessible. Reasons for not adopting MOOCs include lack of student demand, lack of financial resources, and lack of faculty interest (Bischel, 2013; Grajek et al., 2013).

TABLE 1.4 MOOC providers, differentiated by function

MOOC provider type	Description	Examples
Aggregator	An organization that offers courses developed by other education and training providers through a single Internet portal, using a common platform, and with common administration and policies for registration, pricing, and assessment. May be commercial or not-for-profit.	Coursera (commercial); edX (not-for-profit)
Hub	A single Internet portal for access to courses offered by subscribing education and training providers. The platforms and policies of the different courses often vary. (Some hubs call themselves "aggregators" although they do not offer any courses.)	www.class-central.com; www.mooc-list.com
Platform provider	A commercial or not-for-profit organization offering a MOOC platform to others.	Coursera (commercial); edX (not-for-profit): code.edx.org; openmooc.org
University	Some universities and colleges offer courses themselves, from their own platform, or using a third party platform. In the latter case, they might also subscribe to a hub. Many universities offer their courses through an aggregator.	Harvard University, as HarvardX through edX; Nanyang Technological University, through Coursera; University of Tasmania, listed at mooc-list.org
Training providers	MOOCs are popular with training providers, some of which are simply relabeling existing online courses as "MOOCs," while others are revising or developing new courses following developments in MOOC pedagogy. Because they have existing platforms, many training providers continue to use their own platform rather than an aggregator's. Both commercial and not-for-profit training providers are using MOOCs.	www.open2study.org (not-for-profit); NMC Academy, academy.nmc.org (not-for-profit); www.udacity.com (commercial)
Publishers	Publishers are not (yet) providing MOOCs, but they provide content and services for MOOCs.	
University academics	Universities rely on the interest, and often the goodwill, of academics whose participation in MOOC design and development is rarely remunerated above their normal salary.	Academics who author and teach courses offered on edX and Coursera; academics who offer courses directly through iversity.org
Trainers	Trainers who develop MOOCs might offer them through training providers or directly through aggregators, especially if they have used the aggregator's platform to develop the course.	

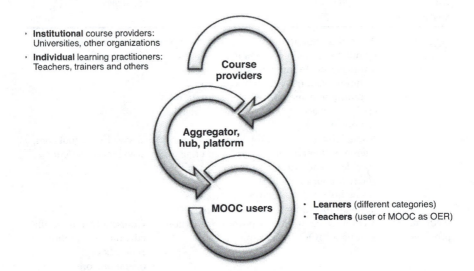

- **Institutional** course providers: Universities, other organizations
- **Individual** learning practitioners: Teachers, trainers and others

Course providers

Aggregator, hub, platform

MOOC users

- **Learners** (different categories)
- **Teachers** (user of MOOC as OER)

FIGURE 1.5 The two-sided market for adoption and acceptance of MOOCs

Fewer than 5 percent of higher education institutions had adopted MOOCs by 2013, even though most offer some form of online learning, which they consider of strategic importance (Allen & Seaman, 2013; Grajek et al., 2013). Another 9 percent of US institutions were considering developing MOOCs in the future (Allen & Seaman, 2013). There is some indication that the rate of MOOC adoption by universities (as providers) is slowing (Marcus, 2013).

A number of commercial training providers seem to be taking advantage of the MOOC "bandwagon." Some offer courses as MOOCs, even though they cannot be accessed or followed without payment. Others, along with some universities, offer courses which are neither massive nor open in formats, labeled SPOCs (Small Private Online Courses).[5]

Individual Learning Practitioners

Learning practitioners include the educators and teachers who develop and run MOOCs. MOOCs also rely on instructional designers and technical developers, who guide and work alongside teachers throughout the design and development process, and assist with practical aspects of using educational technology to prepare educational resources and learning activities (Edinburgh University MOOC Teams, 2013; Head, 2013).

Educators seem to be either MOOC enthusiasts or MOOC skeptics (Haggard & others, 2013). Enthusiasm is most often reported in the general press (Haggard & others, 2013). Enthusiastic MOOC teachers are often excited by learner diversity and what they learn from MOOC development that they can transfer to their other courses; this does not mean, however, that they are blind to the constraints and challenges of teaching with MOOCs (Di Meglio, 2013).

Enthusiastic educators can become discouraged by the course development process if sufficient support is not available. Head (2013) spoke of her frustration before finding the right technical skills for her team: "in recent weeks I've begun to feel naive, and even at times misled, about the necessary resources and procedures." She went on to explain the importance of an instructional designer who understands both the capabilities and the limitations of learning technology.

The two main concerns of MOOC skeptics are perceived shortcomings in pedagogy and a fear that introduction of MOOCs will result in harm. Criticisms of pedagogy refer to the simplistic way in which many xMOOCs, and associated mechanisms for assessment, have been implemented; skeptics tend not to see possibilities for using MOOCs in more sophisticated ways.[6] MOOC skeptics also argue that, among other things, MOOCs may foster plagiarism and perpetuate hierarchy and class differences (Kolowich, 2013; Murphy et al., 2014; Stohl, 2014). Furthermore, they are concerned that academic posts will be lost when educational administrators replace local classroom-based teaching with centrally sourced, low-cost[7] MOOCs (Kolowich, 2013). Criticisms are not leveled at the actual technological or pedagogical advances that underpin and accompany MOOCs, suggesting that the innovation and learning about teaching and learning associated with MOOC development is not an issue.

MOOC Users

A full discussion of MOOC users, their expectations and needs, and their responses to MOOCs would require an entire chapter, if not a book. This section provides a brief overview of current knowledge about the people who register for MOOCs and a summary of user response to MOOCs.[8]

Not all those who register for MOOCs are learners. A first distinction can be made between different levels of participation. As illustrated in Figure 1.6, there are, in decreasing numbers by group: Registrants, who register for a MOOC but do no more; Scanners, who scan some materials without downloading or participating; Downloaders, who download materials but do not participate; Passive Participants, who follow at least part of the first session, but do not complete the first quiz or any other learning activity; Active Participants who complete only the first activity; Active Participants who participate for a longer period without completing the course; Finishers who complete the course but do not request a certificate of completion; Finishers who complete the course and request a certificate or digital badge; and Finishers who complete the course and request verified assessment of their grade. It is possible to follow some courses without submitting any assessments or the outcomes of other activities. Students who "audit" a course in this way might participate at any level from downloading materials only to finishing the course without requesting a certificate, although

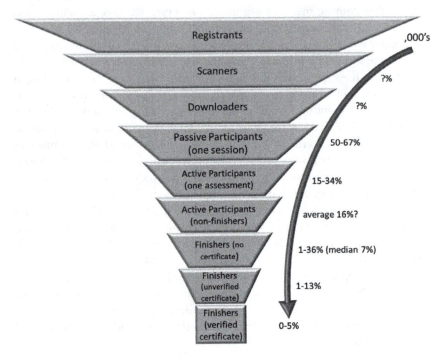

FIGURE 1.6 The MOOC participation funnel: nine categories of participation with decreasing participation rate (not to scale)

Source: The authors, from data in Ho et al. (2014); Jordan (2014); Koller et al. (2013); Murphy et al. (2013); others, see note 10.

auditing is normally considered synonymous with following the course through to the final session.

The reasons for differing levels of MOOC participation are not known. The very high number of inactive registrants in some early MOOCs might, for example, have reflected lack of information about course objectives and content prior to registration (Grimmelmann, 2014). It is not uncommon for registrants who download materials, and are happy to learn from them in their own time, to disagree with media criticisms of low MOOC completion rates, saying that they never intended to take the course in the first place. The large proportion of registrants who audited the MOOCs studied by Kizilcec, Piech, & Schneider (2013) was considered an important, legitimate group of MOOC takers, even though they did not complete the assessments. Retention rates are considered unsuitable indicators of MOOC quality and student satisfaction; proposed alternative indicators based on registration and participation include the percentage of those students who completed the first session who complete the full course, the number of downloads of each resource, and the number of posts to the discussion forum (Ho et al., 2014; Jordan, 2014; Koller et al., 2013).

MOOC registration data can be broken down by geographical location, gender, level of education, and age.[9] The typical MOOC registrant is a male degree holder, aged over 26, from the US.[10] Although the geographical reach of MOOCs is vast, most registrants are in highly populated countries with English-language education systems.

Although progress is being made in measuring registration, participation, and use of MOOC content, less is known about motivations for registration, participation, and progress through MOOCs; which tools and techniques are more or less successful for engagement and learning than others (Reich & Ho, 2014); and how satisfied MOOC users are with their experiences.

Our analysis of the demographic and case study literature suggests the existence of several groups of users with different motivations. Table 1.5 provides an overview, with an indication of what participants in each group expect from MOOC participation. MOOC learners include school students, university students, and life-long learners; many in this last group already have a university degree. Professional educators are a distinct and separate group of MOOC learners and may have accounted for a substantial proportion of early MOOC activity. The table distinguishes between hedonic motivations, i.e., reasons that are primarily associated with the pleasure and experience of MOOC participation, and utilitarian motivations, i.e., those purely associated with the instrumental returns gained from participation or, in some cases, completion.

TABLE 1.5 Groups of learners who participate in MOOCs, their motivations, and their expectations (highlighted expectations are most widely held)

Motivations	Users			
	Learners			Professional educators
	Still at school	At university	Life-long learner (any age, any stage)	
Hedonic	Knowledge-centered Badges, medals	Knowledge-centered as supplement to formal studies	Knowledge-centered Badges, medals are fun for some	Knowledge
Utilitarian		Blended learning (at teacher's direction) NO demonstrated demand for credit	Certified Continuing Education Certificates (badges, medals)	Personal development Source of content

Most cells in Table 1.5 describe participation from which learner expectations can be met without actual completion of the MOOC. The available reports indicate that the most strongly held reason for learner participation in MOOCs is to gain knowledge. Digital badges and medals provide hedonic motivation for some school students and life-long learners, but do not appear to be major motivators. The most significant market for certification appears to be certified continuing education, particularly in the information and communications technology field. The few available studies of university student demand for MOOCs have demonstrated little demand for MOOCs for credit, but professional educators have been vocal users of MOOCs for utilitarian purposes. As well as using MOOCs for their own professional development, teachers use MOOCs as learning resources for homework, blended learning, or in flipped classrooms, as noted earlier.

The rate of learner adoption of MOOCs appears to be decreasing (Baker, 2012; Jordan, 2014; Marcus, 2013). We do not know, however, why such a change might occur. Is it learner dissatisfaction, saturation of initial curiosity, or some other cause? As with any other mode of learning, it is not the mode that makes a good course, but how the course is designed, developed, and run. In the absence of regulation and external quality control and with no requirement for systematic course or teacher evaluation, word of mouth can be expected to play a role in diffusing information about quality of courses, providers, aggregators, and platforms—as it does with other Internet phenomena. In comments and on social media, MOOC participants have been as vocal in their criticisms as in their enthusiasm for their courses. Some MOOCs are appreciated for the care and attention that teachers have taken to prepare engaging and interesting courses, while others are criticized for lack of organization and responsiveness to students.

Conclusion

MOOCs are new and innovative. New types of teaching and learning platform draw on developments in information and communications technology, and online and distance learning, to enable very large numbers of students to participate in courses over the Internet. Innovative types of platform and course provider for the school, post-secondary, adult, and life-long learning markets have emerged to offer MOOCs to a wide variety of users. Massive numbers of learners have registered for, tasted, and successfully completed MOOCs.

MOOCs are also imperfect. While platform capacity for asynchronous learning activities is quite well understood, capacity for synchronous learning activities remains limited even though it can be adjusted "on the fly" to suit some course needs. Despite the potential that platforms and pedagogy offer for development of quite sophisticated open learning courses, many MOOCs offer only simplistic approaches to teaching and assessment. The MOOC marketplace is still developing, and a sustainable configuration of individual, institutional, and commercial providers is yet to emerge. While very many learners from across the globe have participated in MOOCs, we know very little about their motivations, their experience as learners, their satisfaction with their experience, what they learn, what works, and what does not work.

Nonetheless, regardless of how the marketplace evolves and the current weaknesses of MOOCs are addressed, the innovations in technology and pedagogy made by the MOOC pioneers will be transferable to other types of online, face-to-face, and blended courses. The massive scale of these open courses is also teaching us about evaluation of online open learning, and reminding us that it is important to know about our students and what motivates and engages them, no matter how large the enrolment.

It may turn out that MOOCs may establish a new, separate market, disrupt existing markets for education and training and substitute parts of them, or become just another type of open education resource. Yet, MOOCs at no charge have changed the way the world looks at education and training, and have spurred education and training providers to look at themselves.

Acknowledgement

The University of Western Australia provided essential bibliographical support for preparation of this chapter.

Notes

1 Not all MOOCs incorporate all of these advances.
2 *Connectivism* is a learning theory developed by George Siemens (2005). In 2008, he jointly facilitated the first MOOC—on connectivism—with Stephen Downes. According to connectivists, knowledge is distributed across networks of people, things, and the connections among them. The educator's role is to guide socially connected learners to make sense of and learn about the distributed nature of knowledge, and about connections and paths to knowledge.
3 MOOCs that adopt connectivist principles. See note 2 for more detail about connectivism.
4 Author estimate, based on analysis of the Web sites of organizations, listed at www.mooc-list.com at 1 March 2014.
5 Small and Private being the opposite of Massive and Open, SPOCs are excluded from the scope of this chapter. The use of the term, however, suggests that the technical and pedagogical developments that accompany MOOCs will influence approaches to other types of online course.
6 There could be many reasons for simplistic implementation of courses on xMOOC platforms, ranging from limitations in the affordances of xMOOC platform interfaces, to lack of teacher experience in design and building of online courses, to lack of time to produce a more sophisticated course, and more.
7 To the adopting university.
8 We have not included a full list of references to the many case studies and press articles about MOOC use in this section. References to studies reviewed to the time of writing can be obtained from the authors. Two sources to watch for new reports and evaluations are edX's *Research & Pedagogy* page (www.edx.org/research-pedagogy) and

the MOOC Research Institute's *Evidence Hub* (www.moocresearch.com/research-evidence-hub/information, to be populated with the results of research funded by the Bill and Melinda Gates Foundation and other resources in 2014).
9 Statistics about characteristics such as physical and intellectual disability are not currently reported.
10 Aggregated information from several sources was used to reach this conclusion—see note 8.

References

Allen, I. E., & Seaman, J. (2013). *Changing Course: Ten Years of Tracking Online Education in the United States*. Babson Survey Research Group. Boston. Retrieved January 16, 2014, from www.onlinelearningsurvey.com/reports/changingcourse.pdf

Baker, J. W. (2000). The "classroom flip": Using web course management tools to become the guide by the side. In J. A. Chambers (Ed.), *11th International Conference on College Teaching and Learning* (pp. 9–17). Jacksonville: Florida Community College at Jacksonville.

Baker, T. J. (2012). *My CCK11 Experience*. CreateSpace Independent Publishing Platform.

Bischel, J. (2013). The state of e-learning in higher education: An eye toward growth and increased access—Data tables. *ECAR Research Hub*. Louisville, CO: EDUCAUSE Center for Analysis and Research.

The Chronicle of Higher Education. (2013, March). The minds behind the MOOCs: Additional results from The Chronicle's survey. *The Chronicle of Higher Education*. Retrieved January 16, 2014, from http://chronicle.com/article/The-Professors-Behind-the-MOOC/137905/#id=results

Cormier, D. (2008, October 2). The CCK08 MOOC: Connectivism course, 1/4 way. Retrieved January 16, 2014, from http://davecormier.com/edblog/2008/10/02/the-cck08-mooc-connectivism-course-14-way/

Di Meglio, F. (2013, July 25). Are MOOCs the beginning of the end for B-schools? Retrieved January 16, 2014, from www.businessweek.com/articles/2013–07–25/are-moocs-the-beginning-of-the-end-for-b-schools

Downes, S. (2009, February 16). Access 2OER: The CCK08 way. Retrieved January 16, 2014, from http://halfanhour.blogspot.com.au/2009/02/access2oer-cck08-solution.html

Edinburgh University MOOC Teams. (2013, May 10). MOOCs @ Edinburgh 2013 Report # 1. Retrieved January 16, 2014, from www.era.lib.ed.ac.uk/bitstream/1842/6683/1/Edinburgh%20MOOCs%20Report%202013%20%231.pdf

Eisenmann, T., Parker, G., & Van Alstyne, M. W. (2006). Strategies for two-sided markets. *Harvard Business Review, 84*(10), 92–101.

Fisher, C. (2012, November 16). Warming up to MOOCs. *The Chronicle of Higher Education*. Retrieved January 16, 2014, from http://chronicle.com/blogs/profhacker/warming-up-to-moocs/44022

Forsey, M., Low, M., & Glance, D. (2013). Flipping the sociology classroom: Towards a practice of online pedagogy. *Journal of Sociology, 49*(4), 471–485. doi: 10.1177/1440783313504059

Gibbons, J. J. (1986). *The Ecological Approach to Visual Perception*. Hillsdale, NJ: Lawrence Erlbaum Associates.

Grajek, S., Bischel, J., & Dahlstrom, E. (2013). What MOOCs mean to today's students and institutions. Retrieved January 16, 2014, from https://net.educause.edu/ir/library/pdf/ERB1309.pdf

Grimmelmann, J. (2014). *The Merchants of MOOCs*. Digital Commons@UM Carey Law. University of Maryland Francis King Carey School of Law. Retrieved March 28, 2014, from http://digitalcommons.law.umaryland.edu/cgi/viewcontent.cgi?article=2433&context=fac_pubs

Guo, P. J., Kim, J., & Rubin, R. (2014). *How video production affects student engagement: An empirical study of MOOC videos*. Paper presented at the First ACM Conference on Learning at Scale, Atlanta, GA. http://dx.doi.org/10.1145/2556325.2566239

Haggard, S., & others. (2013). *The Maturing of the MOOC: Literature Review of Massive Open Online Courses and Other Forms of Online Distance Learning*. London: UK Department for Business Innovation & Skills. Retrieved January 6, 2014, from www.gov.uk/government/uploads/system/uploads/attachment_data/file/240193/13–1173-maturing-of-the-mooc.pdf

Head, K. (2013, April 3). Sweating the details of a MOOC in progress. *The Chronicle of Higher Education*. Retrieved December 4, 2013, from http://chronicle.com/blogs/wiredcampus/sweating-the-details-of-a-mooc-in-progress/43315

Ho, A. D., Reich, J., Nesterko, S. O., Seaton, D. T., Mullaney, T., Waldo, J., & Chuang, I. (2014). *HarvardX and MITx: The first year of open online courses, fall 2012-summer 2013*. HarvardX and MITx Working Paper. SSRN Working Paper. doi: http://dx.doi.org/10.2139/ssrn.2381263

Hunt, T., & Mares, N. (2013, March 22–April 25). Australian MOOC platform launched using Moodle. Retrieved January 6, 2014, from https://moodle.org/mod/forum/discuss.php?d=225087#p977569

Illich, I. (1971). *Deschooling Society*. London: Marion Boyars.

Jordan, K. (2014). Initial trends in enrolment and completion of massive open online courses. *The International Review of Research in Open and Distance Learning, 15*(1), www.irrodl.org/index.php/irrodl/article/view/1651

Kizilcec, R. F., Piech, C., & Schneider, E. (2013). *Deconstructing disengagement: Analyzing learner subpopulations in Massive Open Online Courses*. Paper presented at the Third International Conference on Learning Analytics and Knowledge, LAK 2013, Leuven, Belgium. http://rene.kizilcec.com/wp-content/uploads/2013/09/Kizilcec-Piech-Schneider-2013-Deconstructing-Disengagement-Analyzing-Learner-Subpopulations-in-Massive-Open-Online-Courses.pdf

Koller, D., Ng, A., Do, C., & Chen, Z. (2013, June 3). Retention and intention in Massive Open Online Courses: In depth. *EDUCAUSE Review*. Retrieved January 16, 2014, from www.educause.edu/ero/article/retention-and-intention-massive-open-online-courses-depth-0

Kolowich, S. (2013, May 2). Why professors at San Jose State won't use a Harvard professor's MOOC. *The Chronicle of Higher Education*. Retrieved January 6, 2014, from http://chronicle.com/article/Why-Professors-at-San-Jose/138941/

Lee, E. (2013, September 22). Science networking service Guokr joins translation project of MOOC platform Coursera. *TechNode*. Retrieved January 6, 2014, from http://technode.com/2013/09/22/science-networking-service-guokr-joins-translation-project-of-mooc-platform-coursera/

Marcus, J. (2013). MOOC bandwagon shows signs of slowing down. *Hechinger Report*. Retrieved January 16, 2014, from http://hechingerreport.org/content/mooc-bandwagon-shows-signs-of-slowing-down_13232/

Martin, S., & Gil, L. (2013). *The OpenMOOC project: Platform based on free software for an open education*. Paper presented at the TNC2013, Innovating Together, Maastricht, The Netherlands. https://tnc2013.terena.org/core/presentation/59

Melcher, M. (2008, September 6). CCK08 first impressions. Retrieved January 16, 2014, from http://x28newblog.blog.uni-heidelberg.de/2008/09/06/cck08-first-impressions/

Murphy, J., Kalbaska, N., Williams, A., Ryan, P., Cantoni, L., & Horton-Tognazzini, L. (2014). Massive open online courses: Strategies and research areas. *Journal of Hospitality and Tourism Education, 26*(1), 39–43.

OECD Centre for Educational Research and Innovation. (2007). *Giving Knowledge for Free: The Emergence of Open Educational Resources*. Paris: OECD Publications.

Parr, C. (2013, April 18). How was it? The UK's first Coursera MOOCs assessed. *Times Higher Education*. Retrieved January 16, 2014, from www.timeshighereducation.co.uk/news/how-was-it-the-uks-first-mooc-assessed/2003218.article

Reich, J., & Ho, A. D. (2014, January 23). The tricky task of figuring out what makes a MOOC successful. *The Atlantic*. Retrieved March 24, 2014, from www.theatlantic.com/education/archive/2014/01/the-tricky-task-of-figuring-out-what-makes-a-mooc-successful/283274/

Siemens, G. (2005). Connectivism: A learning theory for the digital age. *International Journal of Instructional Technology and Distance Learning*. Retrieved January 6, 2014, from www.itdl.org/Journal/Jan_05/article01.htm

Siemens, G. (2012, July 25). MOOCs are really a platform. *eLearn space*. Retrieved January 6, 2014, from www.elearnspace.org/blog/2012/07/25/moocs-are-really-a-platform/

Stohl, C. (2014). Crowds, clouds and community. *Journal of Communication, 64*(1), 1–19.

Yuan, L., & Powell, S. (2013). MOOCs and Open Education: Implications for Higher Education: A White Paper. Retrieved January 6, 2014, from http://publications.cetis.ac.uk/2013/667

2

MOOC PEDAGOGY

Sian Bayne and Jen Ross

Introduction

This chapter addresses an aspect of the rise of the Massive Open Online Course (MOOC), which has had a tendency to be under-discussed in research, reportage and commentary to date: the question of pedagogy. What does it mean to 'teach' in courses in which enrolments can be in the hundreds of thousands? How is the art of course design played out within highly mediated learning spaces, in which the usual institutional and disciplinary rules of the game are radically shifted? What kinds of demands and expectations are brought to bear on university teachers who choose to engage with MOOC design and delivery? And what kinds of discourses and assumptions currently circulate regarding what we can expect of MOOC form, ethos and teaching quality?

We address these questions in two main sections: the first gives an overview of current debates around MOOC pedagogy within the published and popular literatures; the second offers three 'case studies' of individual MOOCs, focusing here on the situated practices of MOOC teachers, and demonstrating how these MOOCs are illustrative of some of the tensions and themes emerging in the literature.

We end with a conclusion that outlines three key themes played out through the literature review and the cases:

1. MOOCs are multiple: we can no longer define them either as a single 'transformative' entity or clearly position them in terms of binary types.
2. MOOC pedagogy is not embedded in MOOC platform, but is negotiated and emergent, a sociomaterial and discipline-informed issue.
3. 'The teacher' persists in the MOOC: though re-worked and disaggregated, the teaching function and teacherly professionalism remain central.

A view from the literature

We begin by exploring something of the diversity of approaches to MOOC pedagogy and design that are being described and commented on by educational researchers and subject specialists. This diversity is framed around three key and emerging issues for MOOC pedagogy:

- A move away from the binary distinction between cMOOC and xMOOC.
- Ongoing debate over MOOC participation patterns.
- A greater emphasis on MOOC platforms than teachers.

There are many areas of the MOOC literature that are not covered here: our aim is to restrict the discussion to issues of pedagogy, which we see as being of particular current importance within the field. Our review of the literature is based on an analysis of MOOC-related journal articles, book chapters and conference papers, supported by a selection of some of the many blog posts, magazine and newspaper articles that have been describing and analysing the MOOC phenomenon. All the material included addresses some aspect of MOOC design, assessment and learning; the emphasis here is on MOOC pedagogy and the impact of MOOCs on teachers and teaching.

Beyond 'cMOOC' and 'xMOOC'

The most influential categorisation of MOOC pedagogy has to date related to the notion that there are two main kinds, each of which determines a particular pedagogical approach: the connectivist or 'cMOOC', driven by principles of pedagogic innovation within a richly networked, disaggregated mode of social learning; and the institutionally-focused 'xMOOC', characterised by a pedagogy short on social contact and reliant on video-lecture content and automated assessment. This simplistic categorisation has hardened into a binary, which – in spite of the variety and complexity in MOOC pedagogies in evidence – continues to offer an overly easy shorthand for describing MOOC provenance and teaching approach.

cMOOCs were the first massive open online courses, designed to test the principles of 'connectivism', working within a framework developed by Downes (2008) and Siemens (2005) to attempt to explain the nature of learning in highly networked environments. Early cMOOCs were designed to foster processes of 'aggregation, relation, creation, and sharing' (Kop 2011) among distributed groups communicating and collaborating online. Arguably, the 'massive' in these courses tends to refer mainly to the scale of the connections, content generation and participant activity in these courses, not their number of participants, which appears to be relatively low in comparison to first waves of xMOOCs.

The term 'xMOOC' was coined to differentiate these cMOOCs from the newer, more massive, institutionally-driven and content-focused courses offered through platforms such as edX (from which the xMOOC gets its name), and Coursera (Downes 2012). xMOOCs are commonly described as being driven by 'behaviourist' principles of knowledge acquisition through repetition and testing (Rodriguez 2012). One argument for this approach is that it can scale up to cater for the numbers of people who sign up for these courses – typical enrolments reach 50,000, while the largest MOOC tracked in one study, Duke University's 'Think Again: How to Reason and Argue', had 226,652 enrolments (Jordan 2013). This scaling up is important to proponents of these larger MOOCs, who often frame their mission as being one of opening global access to education (Knox 2013).

While the cMOOC/xMOOC binary is usefully descriptive of two different trajectories of development, and is much-used by those espousing a connectivist perspective to criticise xMOOCs, recent literature is beginning to move away from what is increasingly seen as a simplistic categorisation, towards more nuanced and micro-level discussion of exactly what is going on in different kinds of MOOCs. This has led some commentators to propose new forms of categorisation (Lukeš 2012; Conole 2013; Lane 2012), and others to propose, for example, the notion of a 'hybrid MOOC' (Waite et al. 2013), or a process by which educators might 'mediat[e] the dichotomy between xMOOC and cMOOC' (Grünewald et al. 2013).

The problem with over-simplistic categorisation of MOOCs is that it may do more than misrepresent what goes on in MOOCs: it may also shape and constrain future MOOC development in unhelpful ways. What we are starting to see now is a move away from the cMOOC/xMOOC binary toward recognition of the multiplicity of MOOC designs, purposes, topics and teaching styles. Some teachers and organisations are rejecting the MOOC acronym altogether, in favour of 'DOCCs: Distributed Open Collaborative Courses' (Jaschik 2013), 'POOCs: Participatory Open Online Courses' (Daniels 2013), 'SPOCs: Small Private Online Courses' (Hashmi 2013) and 'BOOCS: Big (or Boutique) Open Online Courses' (Hickey 2013; Tattersall 2013). Teams and institutions are reframing and reshaping the MOOC and the massive for their own purposes – for collaborations (Scholz 2013), 'flipping' of classrooms (Bruff et al. 2013) and more.

The 'snapshots' offered in this chapter suggest some of the diversity of conceptualisations and designs that underpin MOOCs. Each MOOC is profoundly shaped by its designers, teachers, platform and participants, as we will see. The binary terms 'cMOOC' and 'xMOOC', which are helpful in describing the lineage of MOOCs, are limited in their usefulness for those seeking to develop a MOOC, to understand how MOOCs are actually being experienced, or to draw conclusions about good practice in MOOC design and pedagogy.

Tensions around Participation Patterns

The MOOC participant's role is hotly contested across almost all literature and debate about MOOCs. Indeed, the key dilemmas in MOOCs centre on what participation actually *means*, how it should be measured, and consequently, what metrics of success and quality are appropriate for these courses. These concerns have led to a proliferation of models of participation, including Clow's (2013) 'funnel of participation'; Kizilcec et al.'s (2013) four engagement patterns of completing, auditing, disengaging and sampling (p.3); Hill's (2013) five archetypes of no-shows, observers, drop-ins, passive participants and active participants; Mak et al.'s (2010) dimensions of movement between MOOC environments; and Milligan et al.'s (2013) continuum of 'active', 'lurking' and 'passive' participation.

Such proliferation emerges perhaps because there are simply so many people, doing so many different sorts of things in any given MOOC, that actual practice has to be seen as 'nuanced, strategic, dynamic and contextual' (Mak et al. 2010, p.280). This presents a challenge for researchers, educators and institutions, accustomed to using 'completion' as a fairly stable measure of the success and quality of an educational offering. Formal completion rates (for MOOCs that can measure these), which rarely rise above 10 per cent (Jordan 2013), are increasingly thought not to be the right way to judge the quality of a MOOC or of participants' experiences. The 'outsized media attention' this statistic invariably receives is not taking sufficient account of those who may be engaging but does 'not adhere to traditional expectations, centered around regular assessment and culminating in a certificate of completion' (Kizilcec et al. 2013, p.9).

The notion that people might sign up for a course not intending to complete the assessments is one that is unfamiliar to fee-charging institutions, but it is extremely common in free courses where the barrier to entry is usually as low as clicking a registration button and entering an email address. In such a context, new measures of success and quality are required because participant behaviours and intentions are so diverse.

While presenting researchers with challenges to their assumptions about participation and how to study it (Koutropoulos et al. 2012), Stewart (2013) proposes that this diversity, and the relative freedom to come and go in a MOOC, can be seen as a strength of the format. However, in MOOCs with a connectivist ethos, some forms of participation can be unwelcome. Rather than anxieties about 'completion', which tends not to carry so much significance in these courses (they are rarely formally assessed), in cMOOCs tensions around 'lurking' are pronounced. The idea that people are present, but not actively contributing material to the MOOC, threatens the premise of the cMOOC, which relies on the network to produce, not just to consume, content. 'Lurking' is seen at one extreme to represent a need for more support for participants who may lack confidence (Kop and Carroll 2011), and at the other to be irresponsible and not in the spirit of the MOOC. Arguably, neither of these positions paint the whole picture. The fact that such lurking persists, and at extremely high levels, in cMOOCs has led several authors to suggest that it presents a challenge to the theory of connectivism itself (Bell 2010), while others believe that connectivism can take better account of lurking, while remaining a viable framework (Tschofen and Mackness 2012).

Questions around participation are key in the MOOC research landscape. One set of methods that is seen as useful in achieving a better understanding of MOOC participation is in the emerging domain of learning analytics. The massive data sets that many MOOC platforms generate mean that complex patterns of MOOC participation can be examined, visualised, analysed and discussed in detailed and potentially very fruitful ways. The critical implications of the learning analytic approach are only beginning to be addressed, but they seem to be poised to generate fresh insights into retention, informal learning, feedback and teaching online at massive scale. Indeed, such insights might be relevant in a range of teaching contexts (Scholz 2013). If the necessary critical questions are asked about what can and should be measured by learning analytics (Deimann and Farrow 2013, p.355), they hold considerable promise for longer-term MOOC research and development.

Teachers and MOOCs

The role of the teacher in the MOOC has so far been significantly under-examined. As the authors of a review of the MOOC literature to mid-2012 put it:

> most [MOOC] research has investigated the learner perspective, with a significant minor focus on the institutional threats and opportunities. The lack of published research on MOOC facilitators' experience and practices leaves a significant gap in the literature.
>
> (Liyanagunawardena et al. 2013)

To date, the complexities of teaching on MOOCs have been largely absent from debate, which typically describe only three forms of teacher – the distant 'rock star' or 'academic celebrity' lecturer, the co-participant or facilitator within a network, and the automated processes which serve as proxy tutor and assessor.

The 'academic celebrity' teacher tends to appear in discussions of early MOOCs on the big platforms such as Coursera – the 'xMOOCs'. This role is generally that of respected authority based in an elite institution; not available to MOOC participants in any dialogic or interpersonal way, but primarily through the recordings of their lectures. They take on the role of 'actor-producer' (Rodriguez 2012, p.7). Supplementing this role, 'the teacher' in these MOOCs is also conceived of as a set of automated processes, such as automatically marked quizzes, algorithms for surfacing discussion posts that have been 'upvoted' or read by many participants, and programming tasks that either pass or fail. In some MOOCs these processes are the primary or sole form of feedback to participants. For these reasons, the MOOC is described as being able to operate with 'minimal involvement' from the instructor (Rodriguez 2012, p. 7)

This 'minimal involvement' position is also taken up by cMOOC theorists from another angle. These express the goal of education as facilitating self-directed learning. Expansion of the personal network is considered of primary importance, not just as an 'amplification of learning', but also as a way of overcoming the limited number of teachers (Siemens 2005). Teaching is framed as a supporting device for performing learning. Discussions of teaching in connectivist literature often describe a horizontal 'power-free' domain of participation and sharing (for example McAuley et al. 2010).

In both cases, the individual MOOC as what Grover et al. (2013) describe as a 'designed object' is often not discussed at all, let alone in terms of the philosophies, disciplinary context or choices of a teacher. The pedagogy of the MOOC is commonly held to reside in the platform itself (Knox 2013). Audsley et al. (2013), for instance, describe the 'effective learning methods' built into the design of Coursera (and presumably therefore instantiated in every course taught on the platform) in the following terms:

> Striving to make the platform distinct from other types of MOOCs, the Coursera team sought out sound pedagogy on effective learning methods and then translated the concepts into processes that could be built into the design of the platform itself.
>
> (p.138)

Indeed, Coursera's site describes its 'pedagogical foundations' in some detail, often conflating course design with platform design, for example: 'a key factor in the design of the Coursera system is the extensive use of interactive exercises' (Coursera n.d.). As Feldstein (2012) has put it, what is missing from this account is 'you know . . . teaching'.

However, the minimal involvement position, like the cMOOC/xMOOC distinction, is beginning to be called into question by research examining specific MOOC contexts (Ross et al. 2014). Then, concepts of teacher presence and activity begin to appear, though they may be framed in terms such as 'facilitation' (for example Kop et al. 2011). Mackness et al., analysing the first cMOOC, CK08, describe a necessary role within the MOOC in terms that evoke that of an experienced and skilled teacher, involving a combination of 'light touch moderation', 'firm intervention', and 'explicit communication of what is unacceptable' (Mackness et al. 2010).

Likewise, there is nothing 'minimal' about the ambitions that some describe for the MOOC, and it is difficult to see how the teacher can be constructed as anything other than an active agent in these experiments:

> [MOOCs can] be seen as resources by which institutions can test the delivery models and pedagogies of competitors and themselves, develop new teaching and learning models, and force us to more seriously examine our models and methods of accreditation.
>
> (Anderson 2013)

Teachers we spoke to in the examples that follow described their approaches to, and reasons for, making a MOOC in a whole range of ways, as will be seen. These included: experimenting with scale and complexity; sharing expertise; growing or establishing the profile of their subject area, institution or individual reputation; making education more accessible; and developing new networks. For these, and other reasons, all of these teachers described their engagement with their MOOCs as substantially time-consuming as well as being intellectually and emotionally significant. We predict that the absence of the teacher in the MOOC literature will begin to be remedied as more situated examples of MOOC practice are analysed and discussed.

MOOC Pedagogy: Three Examples

The aim of this section is to further draw out some of the themes raised in the previous section, by looking in more detail at situated teaching practices, understandings of MOOC pedagogy, and the impact of these on teachers who are actively involved in their delivery. Each example is informed by an interview with one or more of the MOOC leads and an attempt to relate teachers' pedagogical approaches both to platform and institutional contexts for the MOOC's delivery. We consider three MOOCs in this section, all issuing from the context of UK higher education:

1   Artificial Intelligence Planning: offered by The University of Edinburgh, via Coursera.
2   Vampire Fictions: offered by Edge Hill University in the UK, using the Blackboard CourseSites platform.
3   Web Science: offered by the University of Southampton, in partnership with FutureLearn.

Artificial Intelligence Planning: Troubling the xMOOC

The Artificial Intelligence (AI) Planning MOOC is included here as one of the first-wave 'xMOOCs' delivered from the UK, via the University of Edinburgh partnership with the US MOOC platform Coursera. As an early UK MOOC on an 'xMOOC' platform, this MSc level MOOC is particularly interesting because of the way it balances the content-focus of conventional 'xMOOCs' with a commitment to community-building, and for its innovative approach to the inclusion of attainment levels within the MOOC design. The MOOC is led by Dr Gerhard Wickler and Prof Austin Tate of the School of Informatics at the University of Edinburgh. It enrolled just under 30,000 participants on its first run in 2013, and is structured around weekly video lectures, optional feature videos, a course discussion forum and classes in Second Life.

Troubling the xMOOC

This course, which, given its discipline area and platform, might have been expected to adopt a content-focused approach to design and a focus on programming skills, was actually driven equally by a desire on the part of the developing team to open up the field of AI Planning to new communities and groupings beyond computing science. In this sense the MOOC design was as much driven by a process- and community-focused ethos as it was by the desire to offer quality teaching content.

Interestingly, part of the motivation for developing this MOOC was a desire on the part of the course team to make a body of rare materials readily available online as part of a legacy approach to a niche collection of teaching material. Professor Austin Tate (see Bayne and Ross 2014) explained that:

> We have a lot of [teaching] materials for occasional use. We were already thinking about how to package that better, particularly as I come to retirement age. We want the materials to be available as a basis for future PhD and MSc student projects. And some material we've got that we didn't want to lose, in particular we've got materials that even some of the originators haven't got any more and we wanted to try and make sure some of that was brought together. So that's the motivation – packaging it well for others to make use of, and the broader we can disseminate that the better.

This teaching material is technical content that has been held by the School of Informatics at the University of Edinburgh for some time, collected over a long period and used occasionally in the teaching of conventional classes, but not until now made widely available online. These materials and their proper care were core to the design ethos of the MOOC.

However, while one driver for the MOOC design was a desire to make available these materials as legacy, an equally strong one was the desire to build and extend a community, as Professor Tate explained:

> The whole framework of it was definitely conceived as, and run as, a community of people interested in a common topic, and working together and exploring that space together. I was trying to reach different communities, and not just those interested in programming.

In part, this was approached by a course design that made success on the course achievable by non-programmers. Participants were able to gain 'Statements of Accomplishment' for achieving one of three 'levels' of successful participation:

- awareness level (aimed at those who were approaching the course as a 'taster' or a very broad introduction to the subject matter – 352 people passed at this level)

- foundation level (for those who had fully grasped the core course content – 148 passed at this level)
- performance level (for those who had taken their understanding of course content to a more advanced level by completing programming assignments or the creation of a digital artefact – 152 passed at this level).

(Tate 2013)

This MOOC did important work therefore in opening up alternative ways of thinking about MOOC 'completion', and in doing so worked to broaden its own community of learners. For example, two science fiction authors took the course at awareness level as a means of achieving a richer subject-knowledge in their literary area. However, it is notable that despite the strong and explicitly-stated commitment to community and collaboration held by the teaching team, levels of discussion and interaction on the MOOC appear to have been low: only 4 per cent of active participants contributed to the discussion forum (Edinburgh 2013) and participation in the Second Life meeting space involved only a few people. Even assuming that some participants were engaging in other media beyond the boundaries of Coursera, the figure indicates that there were high numbers of students engaging in the course primarily via consumption of content and completion of the automatically-marked quizzes.

One reason for this, perhaps, is that the perceived 'norm' of 'xMOOC' engagement as lecture consumption and automated quiz or programming assignment completion was established within early courses dedicated to computing science, and that this is a mode which is both expected and found to be relatively effective within the disciplinary contexts of informatics and engineering. Many students would have enrolled on the course with this expectation. Indeed, the low levels of discussion activity do not correlate either to levels of teacher input, which was high, or to participants' overall satisfaction with the course (on the contrary, in the course evaluation survey (Tate 2013) 93 per cent of respondents found the course excellent, very good, or good).

Further, the Coursera platform (along with Udacity) was originally developed on the basis of the highly successful early MOOCs offered by Stanford University in Machine Learning, Introduction to Artificial Intelligence, and Introduction to Databases. While this disciplinary orientation of the platform is shifting as MOOCs in the Humanities and Social Sciences become more common, it is not unreasonable to suggest that the platform itself still embodies, to an extent, a pedagogical ethos that works well for certain disciplines and teaching philosophies, and less well for others. Thus the social, collaborative intention of the AI Planning MOOC – while impressive – was perhaps working against both disciplinary expectation and the driving platform dynamic, which in the end were the dominant factors in structuring participants' interactions with the course.

Time and Teacher Visibility

Another issue worthy of discussion in relation to the AI Planning MOOC is the teacher time commitment that was given not just to its development, but also – and contrary to some early expectations of MOOC performance – to its delivery. The University of Edinburgh report on their first-wave MOOCs estimates that 'around 30 days of academic (faculty) time is required for a 5–6 week MOOC, plus support and coordination time and direct costs (mainly video production and copyright clearance)' (Edinburgh 2013, 9). Professor Tate noted that the AI Planning MOOC took more time than this average and commented on this time commitment in the following terms:

> It was a bit too intense what we did, too heavy a workload as well. We really were very actively there . . . [it was] challenging in terms of time management . . . I'm still getting complaints about the 6 months we didn't get on holiday!
>
> . . .
>
> You've got to appreciate how long this stuff takes . . . Be prepared to continue to engage and be part of the community while you're doing it.

This significant time commitment is not viewed negatively by the academic staff delivering these early MOOCs – in fact, the teachers we spoke to tended to describe the time-intensive interactions with their courses as energising and addictive. For Professor Tate 'it was a stimulating time, stimulating rather than stressful'. However, as MOOCs become more mainstream components of academic activity, institutions will need to find ways of accounting for the workload they imply, particularly given that MOOC teachers in general appear to want to be highly visible and active in their courses, rather than merely video presences:

> It's not about 'the material is there and you guys need to just get on with it', when I've heard those comments about how we can reduce the cost of doing this, I just don't see this. I think we've got to be actively involved and be seen to be actively involved as the teachers on the course.

In summary then, the AI Planning MOOC usefully plays out some of the key themes emerging from the literature review. The pedagogic approach taken by the academic team designing it was one strongly driven by social learning, and was not constrained by 'conventional' xMOOC design (video lecture, automated assignment). However, despite a clearly successful course in terms of learner satisfaction, the community ethos the designers were aiming for seemed to be tempered by participants' engagement with disciplinary norms and platform constraints, with levels of social interaction being quite low. Here we see a good example of MOOC pedagogy not as something 'designed-in' by the teacher or determined by the platform, but as something emergent and negotiated across multiple sites: teacher intention, teacher philosophy, platform and disciplinary constraint.

'Vampire Fictions' and the Pedagogy of the Undead

The 'Vampire Fictions' MOOC is offered by Edge Hill University in the UK, and led by Dr Ben Brabon. It ran for twelve weeks from September 2013 using the Blackboard CourseSites platform. The number of enrolees was around 1,000, though by mid-way through the course active participants were numbering around 31. The course was organised around weekly readings and video lectures, a discussion forum and a weekly one-hour live classroom.

The 'Vampire Fictions' MOOC is interesting in the UK context in that it is only the second UK MOOC to offer credit (the first being 'First Steps into Learning and Teaching in Higher Education' offered by Oxford Brookes University), and is offered without partnership with a MOOC provider. It is currently the only institutional MOOC offer from Edge Hill University. While designed with the collaborative, social intent of the 'cMOOC' in mind, it is delivered in a relatively structured and content-driven form through CourseSites.

A Pedagogy of the Undead

The 'Vampire Fictions' course seems to have been characterised by forms of haunting. Most notably, this applies to the course design, which Dr Brabon describes as being driven by a 'connectivist' intent, but – largely because of institutional quality and accreditation concerns – became informed by more instructivist and outcomes-driven 'xMOOC' characteristics. He felt that there was 'a sense of haunting, at every level, from the platform through to delivery'. The MOOC design was a kind of 'hybrid', a 'cMOOC' haunted by the 'xMOOC' form:

> When it comes to credit and quality I think there really is a point where an xMOOC pedagogy comes back in, intervenes, almost pricks the surface, punctures the surface ... If you open something completely up how do you guarantee that that self-regulated, open approach meets those learning outcomes, hits the benchmark statements?
>
> (Brabon 2014)

The 'haunting' of this MOOC was also played out here in the sense that the MOOC ethos and pedagogy was tightly influenced by its subject matter, and by Dr Brabon's passion for his subject specialism. The Gothic is the 'point of inspiration' for the teaching strategy of the course: 'As a genre it encourages us to explore our personal fears, anxieties and traumas, through monsters, through vampires.' This subject-informed take on pedagogy, based on individuals' passion for their disciplines, was common across the MOOCs we looked at, and gave a far more interesting inflection to the question of MOOC course design than the identification with 'social constructionism', 'connectivism', 'xMOOC' or 'cMOOC', which tends to focus discussion on the literature. Here, it led to an understanding of a pedagogy very specific to this particular MOOC and the intellectual orientations of its teacher:

> Teaching the undead is a very useful pedagogical strategy, because it pervades different areas of understanding from the medical sciences through to literature, so I think there is something there in terms of its capacity to cross boundaries, to engage the imagination. We all have particular fears, traumas. Teaching the undead — I think there is tremendous scope there.

A Teacher Who Exists

This subject specificity informed Dr Brabon's perception of his own role as a MOOC teacher in that he emphasised his desire not to be there as a 'celebrity academic' but 'as an individual who has a shared enjoyment of vampire fiction: that was key to my thinking about the role of the tutor'. Perhaps another kind of dialogue with the notion of haunting was present in the way in which he emphasised the need to be a 'live' teacher, a teacher that 'exists' and is 'visible': the 'live' classroom sessions in Collaborate became a key element of the teaching strategy in this sense:

> The live class time has been a big discussion point because that, for many of them, has been something different, to actually be able to see me, to actually be in class from time to time, and talk around the point with someone who actually exists in that way.

Perhaps in this emphasis on his own visibility it is unsurprising the MOOC has been characterised by a movement away from social media and the CourseSites platform toward more apparently immediate tutor contact: there has been a 'complete migration away from CourseSites [toward] email'. Although the amount of tutor time given to the course – at approximately four hours per week – is comparable to on-campus equivalents, most of this time is spent on one-to-one email contact with individual course participants:

> I would say that my time isn't spent on CourseSites, it's corresponding with students in other forums. I've been surprised how many students will email me. Even students who don't share in discussion, will strike up conversations with me by email . . . Beyond that hour when we're in class, in the Collaborate session, it's been email, it's been email all the time.

Activity on the discussion board of the MOOC is indeed low, with only about 130 posts in total present by Week 5. However, email activity is likely to be as much influenced by the CourseSites interface, which in this configuration offers easy email access to discussion post authors, as it is to the tutor's own commitment to visibility. Again, how pedagogy is performed here is a question of a coming-together of tutor intent and the design of the platform: it is not possible to see the two as anything but tightly connected.

What it means to be a teacher, in this MOOC, is closely linked to what it means to be an academic and a passionately enthusiastic subject specialist. A desire for connection, and to inspire and inform collective thinking within a particular subject area here, drives the performance of the MOOC teacher:

> In terms of me personally, and my institutional context, I certainly am not aiming for celebrity status or a particular brand identity that academics at big research intensive institutions in the UK or the States already have in place. I think that for me it was more about connecting, connecting with people beyond the walls of the institution, that actually would have common interest and common enjoyment around the reading of vampire and gothic fictions. That I could join into discussion, to inspire and change how we think about this form of fiction. And that was my ambition . . . It was more to do with what I'm doing, than with who I am.

Here then, we see a MOOC pedagogy clearly engages the key themes emerging in the literature review. The MOOC design was very deeply informed by a pedagogy which could not be described in terms of the generic high-level terminologies of 'constructivist', 'connectivist' or 'instructivist' that tend to circulate around discussions of MOOC pedagogy and ethos. Rather, it was a pedagogy which emerged from within a specific disciplinary orientation and set of teacher intentions, but which was then tempered by institutional constraints (the quality assurance processes required for the institution to give the course credit), the platform configuration (which actively pushed learners away from collaborative work with each other toward one-to-one email contact with the tutor), and the dramatic drop-off in levels of participation which pushed the MOOC into the status of a SPOC (small, private online course). Patterns of participation and massive levels of engagement became less important here than the quality of one-to-one support provided by a teacher engaged in supporting a small, credit-bearing course in a niche subject area.

Web Science and the Launch of FutureLearn: Teaching Assemblages and Platform Negotiations

In this example we attempt to take account of what is a significant moment for UK MOOCs: the launch of the UK Open University-led platform FutureLearn.

Here, we take a look at FutureLearn in the period around its launch but before any course completions – an interesting time for discussion, in which the possibilities and potentials for a new way of thinking about MOOCs are foregrounded over outcomes. We interviewed Professor Les Carr at Southampton, who is one of the leads on an early FutureLearn MOOC in Web Science; Professor Carr gives an interesting perspective on what it has meant to design within FutureLearn at this beta stage of its development. We also spoke to Professor Mike Sharples, academic lead at FutureLearn, who was able to provide an overview of the FutureLearn platform and the pedagogic intentions behind its design and launch.

Where's the Pedagogy?: Platform Negotiations

At the time of writing, the FutureLearn platform was undergoing rapid development in the period around launch, and the Web Science course was being built for its first iteration. It was unsurprising, therefore, to find platform issues emerging as a strong theme in discussion with both Professor Sharples and Professor Carr. Professor Sharples emphasised that what is distinctive in the FutureLearn platform design is its difference in pedagogic intent from the US xMOOC platforms with which it might be seen to be competing:

> There is a distinctive pedagogy that's come out of the Open University but also from other university partners in the UK, which is a kind of UK/European pedagogy around social constructivist learning . . . which is distinctive, and to be celebrated and to be understood from a UK perspective.
>
> . . .
>
> And that is different because Coursera, EdX started from a US instructivist approach – you've got star lecturers who want to communicate their understanding to individual learners, and you add some social elements onto that like a forum or a peer assessment, but the notion of large scale social learning isn't underpinning the entire design of those platforms.

It is intriguing, in the context of a globalising phenomenon like MOOCs, to see their ethos and pedagogic principles aligned with characteristics that can be described in terms of nation state and a nationally-held understanding of what constitutes good teaching. We see something similar, on a supra-national scale, with the European platform OpenupEd, the design of which claims to reflect 'European values such as equity, quality and diversity'.[1]

This is perhaps simply indicative of the apparent need within the UK and Europe to define our MOOC offer as distinct from its US equivalents. On the other hand, this notion that MOOC pedagogy can embody a nationally or supra-nationally aligned set of pedagogic principles perhaps does not take account of what we have found to be the heterogeneity of the UK MOOC offer, and the likely heterogeneity of FutureLearn MOOCs themselves. Apparently, discipline-agnostic teaching approaches emerging from the Open University here stand in for – and potentially mask – the variety of teaching approaches developed online and offline within other institutional and disciplinary contexts. However, the transparency and clarity of FutureLearn's approach in building this platform around a specific set of principles – broadly, those of social constructivism – is to be welcomed.

To summarise, and according to the FutureLearn blog (Sharples 2013), principles of social constructivism at scale are designed into FutureLearn via:

- world-class storytelling
- social learning
- celebrating progress.

Thus, while high quality content is clearly important to FutureLearn, the impetus to embed social learning is demonstrated by the tight linking of content with social interaction: discussion forums are associated with content elements rather than grouped separately as we see with other platforms, and a system of reputation-building is embedded within each MOOC. This provides the capacity for each learner to 'follow' other individuals (in a way recognisable to Twitter users), which could work as a strong motivation for learners to maintain the quality of their discussion postings and other interactions, particularly when reputation can be – as is the intention – linked to a learner's record of achievement.

Records of achievement and personal profile pages offer, according to Professor Sharples, a way in for learners to the notion of 'story-telling', enabling them to 'tell the story' of what they have accomplished over the period of the MOOC. Other modes of story-telling include the progress functions built into FutureLearn to indicate 'flow', and allow 'catch-up' and reprise: 'to do' pages, visualisations of progress through the course and a commitment to a general principle of visibility as applied to learner activity and achievement.

However, as we have seen in previous examples, MOOC pedagogy is not something embedded within the platform technical build, but is something that emerges in complex negotiation between platform, the teaching approaches of the academic team developing the course, disciplinary and institutional norms and expectations, and the pattern of learner interactions as the course is played out. In the case of the Web Science MOOC – one of the first to launch through FutureLearn – the pragmatics of managing delivery on time and to the right quality tended to overshadow concern with a pedagogic rationale that perhaps remained implicit. While saying that 'We design learning experiences, then find out we can't do that', because of platform limitations, Professor Carr was relatively sanguine about the limited functionality at this beta stage of platform development, recognising instead the achievement of getting FutureLearn launched. The potential of the platform for offering a new kind of MOOC – one which places good quality content within a framework structured around the social – is clear, even given the relatively pared-back functionality of the beta launch.

At the same time, Professor Carr suggests that some of the more complex activities he would have liked to include could have been achieved by using existing web services outside the MOOC, 'if only you were prepared for handling the complexity of that externally'. This points to an important issue for course developers within all the MOOC platforms, which is the extent to which they keep learner activity within the platform 'walls', and the extent to which they engage with the wider social web. Simplicity in delivery is one motivation for keeping course activity within platform; another is the drive to generate coherent learning analytics. As Professor Sharples pointed out, while FutureLearn is categorically not discouraging people from using existing web-based social media, there is a strong rationale for keeping the social tools within the platform because:

> it means we can also use the analytics that come from that in a number of ways. One, we can provide a learner with a course profile which can be used as part of the assessment process, so it can be a record of achievement which they can then use with employers or for other purposes. And the educators can get a dashboard of what's happening not only with content access but also with social learning, and we can use it for feeding back into the learning design process so we can see what needs to be improved, and what needs to be changed.

On the one hand, the desire to generate meaningful analytics by keeping activity within platform seems quite reasonable; on the other, it would perhaps be a loss if the drive for analytics were to propel online pedagogy back into an earlier era of hermetically-sealed 'VLEs' and a creeping functionalism that neglects the richer serendipities of pedagogic engagement across the wide social web. The opening of FutureLearn content to web searches may go some way toward addressing this question of openness to the wider web.

Network Pedagogy

The necessity for teacher visibility, something which came through strongly in the previous examples, is accounted for in the FutureLearn platform via a disaggregation of the teaching function in the interests of scalability. So, as Professor Sharples explains, FutureLearn has three active 'teacher roles' built in:

- Educator: 'the person with the expertise, the star performer . . . the visible face of the course'.
- Host: 'the one who is engaging with the students directly and is providing academic input'.

- Mentor: 'their role is to facilitate discussions, and it may well be that some of that mentoring role comes up from the community itself'.

In talking with Professor Carr, an equally disaggregated, though perhaps less hierarchical, configuration of the teacher role emerged. For the Web Science MOOC, the teacher role is performed across a network of involved participants, and is strongly embedded within a particular disciplinary orientation:

> we have an interdisciplinary subject and course that we can plunder both relationships in terms of getting lots of people to participate, and material and curriculum . . . it's something that's coming from the whole network, the Web Science doctoral training centre, so we're all involved in it. We're a community of learners.

Professor Carr emphasised that the teaching role in the Web Science MOOC will be performed equally, though across different registers and in different modes, by: doctoral students taking a role in discussion board support; MOOC participants, many of whom it is anticipated will themselves have expertise in web science; the named 'educators' (Professor Carr and Professor Susan Halford); other academic colleagues contributing to weekly topic areas; and the 'celebrity' academics associated with the course (Professor Dame Wendy Hall and Professor Sir Nigel Shadbolt):

> we have a big interdisciplinary team, so we've engaged the whole network to deliver this thing . . . we've been very keen to show off the fact that what we have in the university is a network of professionals operating at different levels, and some of them are celebrity professors who are around once in a blue moon, and some are lecturers and some of them are research students – they each have a role to play in this MOOC.

The Web Science MOOC therefore offers an intriguing portrait of a MOOC pedagogy emerging iteratively with the development of a MOOC platform. Where the FutureLearn platform embeds and pushes MOOC designers toward a social learning model contained by the platform and a hierarchical configuration of teacher roles, the 'network pedagogy' pursued by the MOOC leads was characterised by a flat hierarchy of teaching function and a desire to push beyond the platform 'walls' to the wider social web.

Conclusion

We pull our insights from the two previous sections together into three main concluding points, each of which we believe has important implications for future MOOC research and practice.

1 MOOCs are multiple

The pedagogic richness and variety of MOOCs has received relatively little attention in the literature, and it is still the case that where MOOC pedagogy is discussed, it has often tended to be flattened out into a binary understanding driven by the xMOOC/cMOOC distinction. MOOCs, as we have seen, are already more than one thing: the proliferation of acronym-play around the term – BOOC, SPOC, POOC, DOCC – is indicative of this sense in which 'the MOOC' is becoming multiple.

As we have attempted to illustrate in this chapter, MOOC pedagogy itself takes multiple forms, and can rarely be tightly aligned either with a purely instructivist, outcomes- and content-oriented ethos, or with an entirely collaborative, social and open approach. In this sense, the cMOOC/xMOOC binary has had its day. Each MOOC weaves its own path through these different ways of 'doing' and enacting MOOC design and delivery, and there is scope both in institutional thinking and research to do more work in drawing out and analysing MOOC pedagogy at the more micro-levels of institutional culture and individual MOOC design. Doing so enables us to focus with more clarity on what we actually mean when we talk about MOOC pedagogy, and to understand in greater depth which factors converge to enable a MOOC pedagogy to be enacted. This relates to the next of our key points.

2 MOOC pedagogy is a sociomaterial and disciplinary issue

MOOC platforms are commonly aligned with particular orientations toward pedagogy. Coursera, for example, promises a pedagogy informed by 'retrieval and testing', 'mastery learning' and 'peer assessment' (Coursera, Pedagogical Foundations), while FutureLearn is designed around a set of social constructivist principles to do with 'storytelling', 'discussion', 'visible learning' and 'community supported learning' (FutureLearn, Why it works). There are precedents for this approach in pre-MOOC virtual learning environment design: for example, Moodle's claim that it is 'guided by a "social constructionist pedagogy"' (Moodle, Philosophy). That platform designers work to a set of established pedagogical principles – and make those explicit – is positive, and there is no doubt that platform design informs the way in which MOOC pedagogy is made material and then played out.

However, we should be wary of overestimating the extent to which particular MOOC pedagogies are embedded in, or even particularly enabled by, MOOC platforms: rather, we need to place emphasis on the many agents and influences that come to bear on the final shape of a MOOC design and pedagogic approach. For example, just drawing on the examples discussed in this chapter, it is clear that multiple social and material influences converge when MOOC pedagogy is enacted: teacher preferences and beliefs, disciplinary influences, patterns of learner expectation and engagement, and other contextual factors such as institutional teaching culture or the desire to generate analytics. Platform functionality and ethos work as one element in the sociomaterial mix, rather than a guarantor of pedagogic coherence. Theories of the sociomaterial can help us here, as practitioners and institutions, in thinking through the ways in which MOOC pedagogies are played out through multiple connections: 'human and non-human, social discourses, activities and meanings, as well as material forces, assemblages, and transformations' (Fenwick et al., p. 2).

Disciplinarity emerged in our case studies as a key influence on MOOC pedagogy. Where the influence of disciplinary culture has been well-researched in the general literature on higher education teaching, learning and research (for example Kreber 2009, Trowler 2008), the MOOC literature has not to date taken it much into account, focusing rather on issues of platform determination or generic discipline-agnostic frameworks like 'connectivism' or 'social constructivism'. Yet we saw pedagogic approaches being very tightly aligned to disciplinary 'ways of thinking and practicing' (McCune and Hounsell 2005), from the 'network pedagogy' of the Web Science MOOC, to the 'pedagogy of the undead' of Vampire Fictions. Modes for community formation and social learning already feature strongly in MOOC literature and debate, but these tend not to be related to disciplinary context or to the role of the teacher as disciplinary guide or gatekeeper. However, if, as Northedge and McArthur (2009) point out, 'higher education can be understood as providing students with interim access to a discipline community' (p. 110), we perhaps need to give more attention to the ways in which these aspects of the social are specific to the disciplinary context of the MOOC. This leads us to our final point, which relates to the function of the teacher in the MOOC.

3 The MOOC teacher persists

The 'teacher function' within the MOOC is disaggregated and re-worked in different ways, depending on platform and pedagogy. Platform-defined roles speak their own definition of how 'the teacher' might be understood, from the 'educator, host and mentor' of FutureLearn, to the 'instructor, teaching assistant and community teaching assistant' of Coursera. Other aspects of the teacher function are informed by more discursive constructions that circulate through practitioner and researcher networks: from the 'facilitator' and 'fellow node' privileged by those drawn to 'connectivist' approaches, to the celebrity academic or role-model suggested by the promise of access to the 'world-class professor' in Coursera (Coursera, About us).

There are two main points to make here. The first is that regardless of how the teacher function is disaggregated and re-described, the need to value the notion of the teacher within the MOOC remains: MOOC teaching is high-visibility, high-risk and dependent on significant intellectual, emotional and time commitment from academics and the professionals who work alongside them. MOOC pedagogy functions, to a significant degree, as a representation of these teachers' disciplinary, pedagogic and personal orientations to the challenging task of course delivery in the open, and at scale.

At the same time, however, we need to be prepared to re-think how certain teacher-functions are enacted in MOOC space, and by whom or what. Machinic substitutions for teacher feedback are already common in MOOCs that apply automatic marking to quizzes and assessments. The 'teacher as code' is likely to become more of a feature, as assessment technologies like Automated Essay Scoring, already subscribed to by the MOOC platform EdX, become common (see Balfour 2013 for a useful review). Intelligent tutoring and adaptive learning systems for MOOCs, informed by advances in natural language processing and learning analytics, are likely to further orient MOOC pedagogy toward the non-human teacher. A challenge here is to balance what is good in machinic intervention in the teaching function with a critical understanding and valuing of the professionalism and pedagogic capacities of the human teacher.

Machinic interventions in the teacher function along the lines of those described above go alongside social interventions and the spreading of this function among communities of learners: when teaching is delivered at massive scale, we need to understand how best to enable learning communities to coalesce around shared matters of concern. From the reputation-building functions of FutureLearn, to the introduction of Community Teaching Assistants in Coursera, and the long-running commitment of the 'cMOOCs' to the patterns and formations of the personal learning network, we see the higher education community engaging with this aspect of the teacher function with energy and commitment. Again, the challenge here is in balancing the nurturing of massive-scale learning community with an understanding of the role of the teacher as an important, and irreplaceable, 'way in' to disciplinary community.

Acknowledgements

This chapter is adapted, with permission, from a report commissioned by the UK Higher Education Academy, whom we wish to thank for funding the research on which it is based. We also wish to thank the colleagues who agreed to be interviewed to inform the case studies presented here: Dr Benjamin Brabon, Professor Austin Tate, Professor Les Carr and Professor Mike Sharples.

Note

1   www.openuped.eu/openuped-temp/59-about-openuped

References

Anderson, T., 2013. Promise and/or Peril: MOOCs and Open and Distance Education. Available at: www.col.org/SiteCollectionDocuments/MOOCsPromisePeril_Anderson. pdf [accessed February 11, 2013].

Audsley, S., Fernando, K., Maxon, B., Robinson, B. and Varney, K., 2013. An examination of Coursera as an information environment: Does Coursera fulfill its mission to provide open education to all? *The Serials Librarian*, 65(2), pp. 136–166.

Balfour, S., 2013. Assessing writing in MOOCs: Automated essay scoring and calibrated peer review™. *Research and Practice in Assessment*. 8, pp. 40–48.

Bayne, S. and Ross, J., 2014. *The Pedagogy of the Massive Open Online Course (MOOC): The UK View*. York, UK: The Higher Education Academy.

Bell, F., 2010. Connectivism: Its place in theory-informed research and innovation in technology-enabled learning. *The International Review of Research in Open and Distance Learning*, 12(3), pp. 98–118.

Brabon, B., 2014. Vampire Fictions MOOC (Massive Open Online Course). Available at: www.edgehill.ac.uk/english/courses/vampire-fictions/ [accessed January 20, 2014].

Bruff, D. O., Fisher, D. H., McEwen, K. E., and Smith, B. E., 2013. Wrapping a MOOC: Student perceptions of an experiment in blended learning. *MERLOT Journal of Online Learning and Teaching*, 9(2), 187–199.

Clow, D., 2013. MOOCs and the funnel of participation. In *Proceedings of the Third International Conference on Learning Analytics and Knowledge*. LAK '13. New York: ACM, pp. 185–189. Available at: http://doi.acm.org/10.1145/2460296.2460332 [accessed February 11, 2013].

Conole, G., 2013. A new classification for MOOCs. *MOOC Quality Project*. Available at: http://mooc.efquel.org/a-new-classification-for-moocs-grainne-conole/ [accessed February 11, 2013].

Coursera, Pedagogical Foundations. Available at: www.coursera.org/about/pedagogy [accessed February 11, 2013].

Daniels, J., 2013. MOOC to POOC: Moving from massive to participatory. *JustPublics@365*. Available at: http://justpublics365.commons.gc.cuny.edu/2013/02/05/mooc-to-pooc-moving-from-massive-to-participatory/ [accessed February 11, 2013].

Deimann, M. and Farrow, R., 2013. Rethinking OER and their use: Open education as Bildung. *The International Review of Research in Open and Distance Learning*, 14(3), pp. 344–360.

Downes, S., 2008. An introduction to connective knowledge. In T. Hug, ed. *Media, Knowledge & Education: Exploring New Spaces, Relations and Dynamics in Digital Media Ecologies*. Innsbruck, Austria: Innsbruck University Press.

Downes, S., 2012. Massively open online courses are 'here to stay'. *Stephen's Web*. Available at: www.downes.ca/post/58676 [accessed February 11, 2013].

Feldstein, M., 2012. Everybody wants to MOOC the world. *e-Literate*. Available at: http://mfeldstein.com/everybody-wants-to-mooc-the-world/ [accessed February 11, 2013].

Fenwick, T., Edwards, R. and Sawchuk, P., 2011. *Emerging Approaches to Educational Research: Tracing the Sociomaterial*. Abingdon: Routledge.

Grover, S., Franz, P., Schneider, E. and Pea, R., 2013. The MOOC as distributed intelligence: Dimensions of a framework & evaluation of MOOCs. In *Computer Supported Collaborative Learning 2013*. Madison, WI.

Grünewald, F., Meinel, C., Totschnig, M. and Willems, C., 2013. Designing MOOCs for the support of multiple learning styles. In D. Hernández-Leo, T. Ley, R. Klamma and A. Harrer (eds), *Scaling Up Learning for Sustained Impact*. Lecture Notes in Computer Science. Springer Berlin Heidelberg, pp. 371–382. Available at: http://link.springer.com/chapter/10.1007/978-3-642-40814-4_29 [accessed February 11, 2013].

Hashmi, A. H., 2013. HarvardX set to launch second SPOC. *Harvard Crimson*. Available at: http://harvardx.harvard.edu/links/harvardx-set-launch-second-spoc-harvard-crimson-amna-h-hashmi-september-16–2013 [accessed February 11, 2013].

Hickey, D. T., 2013. 1st 'BOOC' to begin in September, scaling-up what works. *BOOC*. Available at: www.indiana.edu/~booc/1st-booc-to-begin-in-september-turning-point-for-open-online-courses/ [accessed February 11, 2014].

Hill, P., 2013. Emerging student patterns in MOOCs: A (revised) graphical view. *e-Literate*. Available at: http://mfeldstein.com/emerging-student-patterns-in-moocs-a-revised-graphical-view/ [accessed February 11, 2013].

Jaschik, S., 2013. Feminists challenge Moocs with Docc. *Times Higher Education*. Available at: www.timeshighereducation.co.uk/news/feminists-challenge-moocs-with-docc/2006596.article [accessed February 11, 2013].

Jordan, K., 2013. MOOC completion rates. Available at: www.katyjordan.com/MOOC project.html [accessed February 11, 2013].

Kizilcec, R., Piech, C. and Schneider, E., 2013. Deconstructing disengagement: Analyzing learner subpopulations in Massive Open Online Courses. In *LAK '13*. Leuven, Belgium.

Knox, J., 2013. The limitations of access alone: Moving towards open processes in education technology. *Open Praxis*, 5(1), pp. 21–29.

Kop, R., 2011. The challenges to connectivist learning on open online networks: Learning experiences during a massive open online course. *The International Review of Research in Open and Distance Learning*, 12(3), pp. 19–38.

Kop, R. and Carroll, F., 2011. Cloud computing and creativity: Learning on a Massive Open Online Course. *European Journal of Open, Distance and E-Learning*.

Kop, R., Fournier, H. and Mak, J., 2011. A pedagogy of abundance or a pedagogy to support human beings? Participant support on massive open online courses. *International Review of Research in Open and Distance Learning*, 12(7), pp. 74–93.

Koutropoulos, A., Gallagher, M., Abajian, S., de Waard, I., Hogue, R., Keskin, N. and Rodriguez, C., 2012. Emotive vocabulary in MOOCs: Context & participant retention. *European Journal of Open, Distance and E-Learning*, (2). Available at: www.eurodl.org/index.php?article=507 [accessed February 11, 2013].

Kreber, C. (ed.), 2009. *The University and its Disciplines: Teaching and Learning Within and Beyond Disciplinary Boundaries*. New York: Routledge.

Lane, L., 2012. Three kinds of MOOCs. *Lisa's Online Teaching Blog*. Available at: http://lisahistory.net/wordpress/2012/08/three-kinds-of-moocs/ [accessed February 11, 2013].

Liyanagunawardena, T. R., Adams, A. A. and Williams, S. A., 2013. MOOCs: A systematic study of the published literature 2008–2012. *The International Review of Research in Open and Distance Learning*, 14(3), pp. 202–227.

Lukeš, D., 2012. What is and what is not a MOOC: A picture of family resemblance (working undefinition) #moocmooc. *Researchity—Exploring Open Research and Open Education*. Available at: http://researchity.net/2012/08/14/what-is-and-what-is-not-a-mooc-a-picture-of-family-resemblance-working-undefinition-moocmooc/ [accessed February 11, 2013].

Mackness, J., Mak, J. and Williams, R., 2010. The ideals and reality of participating in a MOOC. In *Proceedings of the Seventh International Conference on Networked Learning*. Lancaster: University of Lancaster, pp. 266–275. Available at: www.lancaster.ac.uk/fss/organisations/netlc/past/nlc2010/abstracts/PDFs/Mackness.pdf [accessed February 11, 2013].

Mak, S., Williams, R. and Mackness, J., 2010. Blogs and forums as communication and learning tools in a MOOC. In L. Dirckinck-Holmfeld et al., eds. *Networked Learning Conference*. Lancaster: University of Lancaster, pp. 275–285. Available at: http://eprints.port.ac.uk/5606/ [accessed February 11, 2013].

McAuley, A. et al., 2010. The MOOC model for digital practice. Available at: https://oerknowledgecloud.org/sites/oerknowledgecloud.org/files/MOOC_Final_0.pdf [accessed February 11, 2013].

McCune, V. and Hounsell, D., 2005. The development of students' ways of thinking and practising in three final-year biology courses. *Higher Education*, 49(3), pp. 255–289.

Milligan, C., Littlejohn, A. and Margaryan, A., 2013. Patterns of engagement in connectivist MOOCs. *Journal of Online Learning and Teaching*, 9(2).

Northedge, A. and McArthur, J., 2009. Guiding students into a discipline: the significance of the teachers' knowledge. In Kreber, C., ed. *The University and its Disciplines*. New York: Routledge.

Rodriguez, C. O., 2012. MOOCs and the AI-Stanford like courses: Two successful and distinct course formats for Massive Open Online Courses. *European Journal of Open, Distance and E-Learning*.

Ross, J., Sinclair, C., Knox, J., Bayne, S. and Macleod, H., 2014. Teacher experiences and academic identity: The missing components of MOOC pedagogy. *Journal of Online Learning and Teaching*.

Scholz, C., 2013. MOOCs and the Liberal Arts College. *Journal of Online Learning and Teaching*, 9(2).

Sharples, M. (2013). Social learning and large scale online learning. Available at: https://about.futurelearn.com/blog/massive-scale-social-learning/ [accessed December 15, 2013].

Siemens, G., 2005. Connectivism: A learning theory for the digital age. *International Journal of Instructional Technology and Distance Learning*, 2(1). Available at: www.itdl.org/Journal/Jan_05/article01.htm [accessed February 11, 2013].

Stewart, B., 2013. Massiveness + openness = new literacies of participation? *Journal of Online Learning and Teaching*, 9(2). Available at: http://jolt.merlot.org/vol9no2/stewart_bonnie_0613.htm [accessed February 11, 2013].

Tattersall, A., 2013. Gold Rush or just Fool's Gold—A quick look at the literature. *ScHARR MOOC Diaries*. Available at: http://scharrmoocdiaries.blogspot.co.uk/2013/07/scharr-mooc-diaries-part-xvii-gold-rush.html [accessed February 11, 2013].

Trowler, P. and Wareham, T., 2008. Tribes, territories, research and teaching: Enhancing the teaching-research nexus. Final report. York: The Higher Education Academy. Available at: www.heacademy.ac.uk/projects/detail/projectfinder/projects/pf2966lr [accessed 11 November 2013].

Tschofen, C. and Mackness, J., 2012. Connectivism and dimensions of individual experience. *International Review of Research in Open and Distance Learning*, 13(1), pp. 124–143.

Waite, M., Mackness, J., Roberts, G. and Lovegrove, E., 2013. Liminal participants and skilled orienteers: Learner participation in a MOOC for new lecturers. *Journal of Online Learning and Teaching*, 9(2). Available at: http://jolt.merlot.org/vol9no2/waite_0613.htm [accessed February 11, 2013].

3

TO MOOC OR NOT TO MOOC?

University Decision-Making and Agile Governance for Educational Innovation

Jeff Haywood and Hamish Macleod

The MOOC Ecology

At the time of writing (late 2013/early 2014), our analysis of detailed data provided by Coursera, one of the major MOOC hosting companies and with which we partner, showed some interesting patterns of types of organisations, age of partnership and number of MOOCs offered. Of the 78 organisations in the dataset, 45 per cent joined in the 'early phase', which we are defining as 'before end 2012', and 54 per cent joined in the 'late phase', i.e. January 2013 onwards. By November 2013, the late phase partners had almost all provided between one and seven MOOCs, and only two had offered more (eight MOOCs). Given the time since joining, this observation is unsurprising. However, the early phase partners had also mainly (61 per cent) offered only up to seven MOOCs, and those which had offered more than seven MOOCs were distributed between those offering eight and those offering twenty-seven MOOCs. It appears that some universities have strategies and operational processes/capacities that lead them to develop many MOOCs rapidly; in reality without much time to learn from one group before embarking on the construction of the next group, and others are more 'paced' or more restricted by capacity for production and management.

The University of Edinburgh is in the early phase cohort and has so far offered six MOOCs on Coursera, with a further eight well on the way to completion. We have a capacity limitation on video production, but more importantly, we have a strategic approach to MOOCs that requires us to have a light business case for each that has a reason for creating a MOOC that goes well beyond just another 'me too MOOC'. This requires substantial iteration with each potential MOOC team, and scheduling for video and instructional design. We also wish to cover as wide a range of subjects as possible, and so each MOOC is more distinctive than would be the case for many MOOCs in closely related subjects and we wish to build additional capacity for online learning across the University.

It will be interesting to watch these different types of Coursera partners over the next few years to see if stable patterns of MOOC provision emerge, and also to compare that with partners on other MOOC platforms as these mature.

Types of MOOC Platforms and University Choices for Partnership

Since the appearance of the first companies (we shall use the term 'MOOC platforms') set up to offer MOOCs around 2011–12, there has been a steady rise in the number of these platforms and also in variants of them. These can be classified as follows, with examples of each:

This range of platforms offers choices to potential MOOC providers, mainly universities, as to where to place their open online courses, and of course the option to be 'faithful' to one or 'promiscuous' with several. This choice was very limited (and perhaps simpler) for early MOOC-providing universities, for example in summer 2012, and several MOOC platforms have been set up quite recently (i.e. spring, summer 2013) so it is not surprising that the early entrants have attracted the majority of university partners at the date of writing. Competition between MOOC platforms for MOOC providers and for MOOCs with good monetisation potential will inevitably be one aspect of the decision-making process for

TABLE 3.1 Global MOOCs (2011–2012)

Type of MOOC platform	Selected examples and (country)
Independent company and for profit	Coursera (US)
	Iversity (DE)
	Udacity (US)
Independent company and not for profit	edX (US)
	Futurelearn (UK)
	Open2Study (US)
Government sponsored/owned	France Numerique Universite FUN (FR)
DIY: in-house but open to other universities to add their own content	no examples at present
DIY: in-house but only for self-created content	ALT (UK)
	UK OU (UK)
As extension of existing commercial operation	Blackboard Coursesites (US)
	Google (US)
	Instructure (Canvas) (US)
Portal to in-house MOOCs and VLEs	OpenupEd (NL)
Not for profit organisation with commercial sponsorship/support	MiriadX (ES)

new entrant MOOC providers, and perhaps be an element in any review and reconsideration for those already in the field. Some platforms select their partners carefully from specific groups of universities, especially high ranking ones (e.g. edX, Coursera) and some are open to everyone, university or individual faculty member, to mount courses (e.g. Coursesites, iversity). Thus competition will take different forms, depending upon the open-ness of the platform to universities, colleges and other organisations.

At present, most universities are 'faithful' to one platform, probably mainly because the administrative overheads on working with two or more platforms are significant as we have found at the University of Edinburgh (Coursera and Futurelearn). At present it also isn't clear that any one platform will necessarily be better than another, although each will offer advantages and disadvantages to any given potential partner (e.g. in terms of the digital learning environment interface design, marketing reach, monetisation strategy). With the emergence of 'national MOOC platforms', that is those supported explicitly by governments financially or in speeches (e.g. Futurelearn in UK, FUN in France), a political dimension enters the decision process as funding or other advantages may arise from universities being active on their own national platform, and perhaps handicaps result from not being present, even though those national MOOC platforms are also open to providers beyond their state boundaries. This would be particularly true for universities already active on a platform not in their own country. Another reason for the emergence of MOOC platforms in countries outside the US is where language is felt to be an important issue, for example France and francophone languages, and the Gulf States and Arabic script. The platform itself can be in the language of the majority of MOOCs offered, aiding access to those with limited English. It may be that existing MOOC platforms such as Coursera and Futurelearn may eventually create full multilingual platforms if demand warrants it, with signs of this in the support of multiple alphabets and full translation services. Regardless of the MOOC platform approach, different language groups (e.g. Spanish, French, Mandarin) can self-form within individual MOOCs by individual learners getting together, as we have seen happening in our own MOOCs.

From the perspective of faculty, a major influence on whether they would prefer their MOOC on one platform or another is likely to be the affordances and limitations of the digital learning environment on offer (i.e. the software services and applications provided, open-ness to use of applications outside the platform DLE) and whether they are able to offer their course in the way they would wish. All DLEs contain embedded pedagogical models, and faculty wishing to offer innovative education will have views on whether their platform DLE can or cannot support them.

From the perspective of potential inter-university (inter-provider) collaboration, presence on a single platform is most powerful, and was certainly a significant factor in our decisions at the University of Edinburgh to join Coursera (US peer network) and Futurelearn (UK peer network). It will be interesting to watch how this plays out over the next few years.

MOOC Providers Beyond the Original University Sector

Although so far in this chapter we have considered MOOC providers all to be educational institutions, mainly traditional universities, this situation is changing. While the original entrants in 2012–13 are still present, and are all high ranked universities, the recent entrants are more varied. High rank universities still predominate, although the definition of 'high rank' has expanded to include those at the top end of their own national rankings rather than world league tables such as QS World Rankings. This has enabled a wider range of countries to be represented in the MOOC provider community, and also MOOCs in a potentially wider range of languages to be offered. At present Chinese, French, Russian and Spanish are the most common languages, although several MOOCs have been translated by their learning community into Portuguese.

For lower ranking universities, the offer to join the global MOOC community alongside universities much higher up the league tables must be very attractive. This has caused some debate among the top ranked universities, many of which had joined what they thought would be an 'exclusive club', and one can see some evidence of attempts to manage this challenge within MOOC platform websites. To date it does not appear that any top rank universities have left a platform because of this, nor that they have decided to cease offering MOOCs (although, given the multi-year contracts generally signed with commercial platforms, this will probably take time to become visible); however, it is likely that all universities are reviewing their medium term strategies and the choice of MOOC platforms will be part of that review. The open universities in Europe, which are strong education providers with a track record of open and online education, have come together to offer their own platform, albeit of a portal to MOOCs rather than a single MOOC DLE ('OpenupEd'), and, with the support of the European Commission, this has taken on something of a supra-national MOOC platform role (www.openuped.eu/).

For those working with more than one platform, they will be operating a regular decision process to decide which MOOC is placed where. It is likely that MOOC platforms would prefer, or might even try to mandate, to be the sole platform for any given MOOC, and may indeed seek 'high impact MOOCs' rather than leave that to the provider's preference. The media and press take great interest in this area, looking for dissatisfaction with platforms or partners (Straumsheim, 2013).

Alongside the diversifying university MOOC providers are now also small or specialised higher education institutions (e.g. IE Business School, Berklee College of Music), and agencies/organisations with cultural/educational missions such as the British Library and the World Bank. Some of these join as partners of universities and some join in their own right. It is likely that high ranking organisations in the non-university category will be increasingly sought after by MOOC platforms as the number of high ranking universities which are potential partners decreases. Analysing Coursera data, we can see that so far the majority of partners beyond the original universities are in the US (83 per cent), and a similar profile seems to be emerging with Futurelearn and universities in the UK. So far edX has not recruited beyond the traditional partner base, with perhaps the one exception of a school of music (Berklee), and indeed edX website lists its partners under the heading of 'Schools' (which itself is a very US expression), whereas Coursera, Futurelearn and OpenupEd list theirs under the heading 'Partners'.

Decision-Making in Potential MOOC Providers

Universities and other MOOC providers have generally made limited public statements about their reasons for joining MOOC platforms, although press and media interest in this has brought some information into the public domain (Haywood, 2012). The decision as to whether to offer MOOCs at all, regardless of platform, has clearly been, and remains, high on the agenda for senior management teams in universities around the world. For the major MOOC platforms, it is the institution that joins as a partner, rather than individual faculty, although examples of MOOC platforms open to individual faculty do exist (e.g. Coursesites, iversity) and may be quite problematic for universities to manage risk and reputation if faculty use them. The MOOC management process, centralised versus devolved, mirrors that for open educational content on sites such as YouTube and iTunesU.

As far as we can determine there are two main university approaches to managing MOOC creation and delivery: tight central control and investment versus highly devolved, faculty-led. We might call this the degree of 'institutional cohesion'. In the former cohesion type, in which the University of Edinburgh sits, there is a strong management process that approves, funds, oversees and administers the MOOCs that are proposed by faculty, and indeed may search or 'commission' MOOCs from a strategy viewpoint ('a good MOOC to offer would be . . .'). Most European/UK universities offering MOOCs seem to be of this type, perhaps reflecting this style of management even in quite devolved research intensive universities. A similar process probably also operates in SE Asia and Australia/New Zealand. The mission-led, strategic, risk-management viewpoint is apparent. The US model is generally more of the highly devolved type, reflecting a stronger academic School independence, although even here the need for risk management, funding and central MOOC administration have demanded strong senior management engagement. The contracts with MOOC platforms provide an insight into this dichotomy of responsibility: Is the MOOC the 'property' of the university or the faculty? Who signs off the agreement on the third party

IP liability? Coursera has a tendency towards the individual faculty whereas Futurelearn tends towards the institution.

We see these main general reasons (unranked) to offer MOOCs or to refrain from them. Institution-level reasons for offering MOOCs:

A   Reputation boost as innovative organisation.
B   Potential direct income from MOOCs, e.g. certificates, books.
C   Potential indirect income from MOOCs, e.g. fee-paying student recruitment.
D   Basis for educational R&D for taught online programmes.
E   Basis for educational R&D for on-campus programmes.
F   Stimulates academic debate inside university about pedagogy, online and in the classroom.
G   Stimulates academic debate inside university about future of HE.
H   Opportunity to collaborate with peer universities, locally or internationally.
I   Opportunity to collaborate with key groups/organisations (for example alliances, government agencies, non-governmental organisations).
J   Response to political pressure.
K   Fun! Adds an excitement to learning and teaching.
L   Belief in open education and aligns with existing open activities.
M   Desire to expand outreach to individuals not otherwise accessing (own) university education.
N   Desire to outreach to disadvantaged individuals.

Institution-level reasons against offering MOOCs or for waiting:

O   First mover advantage is waning.
P   Too high risk a venture if (confidence in) local expertise weak.
Q   Faculty/unions are opposed/wary.
R   Board/council opposed/wary.
S   No appropriate platform for pedagogy intended to be used.
T   Minority language university – faculty not competent/confident to teach in major world language.
U   Likely only to produce MOOCs in subjects already in good supply.
V   Cannot see likelihood of large enough audiences.
W   Cannot see adequate return on investment for the effort involved, e.g. opportunity cost of faculty time.
X   Exclusivity of existing platforms, no option to join desired platforms.
Y   Opposed to idea of offering high value educational materials openly due to loss of control.
Z   Regard MOOCs as poor pedagogy, with quality below acceptable standard for university.
AA Lack of funding stream/priority to devote to this activity.

We derived these possible benefits and drawbacks/barriers from a combination of our own analysis of the discussion inside the University of Edinburgh, validated through discussions with wide-ranging contacts across many colleagues inside and outside the MOOC-sphere and through analysis of public documents and statements.

At the University of Edinburgh we have been open about our reasons since the beginning when the press began to ask us questions in the wake of our announcement on joining Coursera, and later Futurelearn (Parr, 2013; Parr, 2014). We felt it was better to have our real reasons in public than have ill-informed and sometimes cynical speculation. Our reasons were, and remain: reputation (A), educational R&D (D, E), outreach (M, N), partnerships and fun (K10). Different members of the university will have their own view of the rank order of these reasons; for the authors D, E and F are uppermost, and with K (fun) as a strong motivator.

Drawing upon public evidence, and on personal conversations and discussions with colleagues in the senior teams of our peer universities, we can see mainly the same reasons being given, although with differing emphases. In some cases, financial return (B and C) was also anticipated beyond that of the cost of developing and delivering the MOOCs, and as a consequence a few universities invested directly in MOOC platforms, for example in Coursera (Stanford University, University of Pennsylvania) and in edX, where Harvard and MIT made multimillion dollar investments. Investing in spin-outs is part of their general approach to commercialisation of faculty and student ideas and funding MOOC platform companies may mostly be an example of following this pattern, although offering wider access to their education is among other reasons given.

Some clear examples exist where high ranking universities have decided not to offer MOOCs, at least for the present, and their reasons appear to be mainly faculty opposition (Q), Board or Council wariness (R), and poor pedagogy in MOOCs (Z). Among the wider university community, especially in countries still trying to (re-)build their higher education, lack of resources/priority (AA) are likely to predominate, with minority language being a barrier for many in non-Anglophone countries until recently (T).

For individual faculty, and their academic departments, some of the reasons for and against will be the same as those for their university as a whole, but in addition we have seen a desire among faculty at Edinburgh and elsewhere to promote their own academic subject more strongly, to achieve some of the status accorded to the early academic entrants ('rockstar'), and a wish to strengthen their CV. We are aware of some anecdotal evidence that being part of a MOOC team has had some personal career benefit for faculty, adjunct faculty and for TAs, and books, charity donations and sustained community networks of interest have also appeared. These spin-offs are likely to grow with time, although early adopter benefits may remain strong.

The reasons why faculty become interested in developing and offering MOOCs are as varied as those of their universities. Through conversations with the faculty involved in our thirty MOOCs, both offered and under development, we can identify the following as the main reasons for involvement, with more than one applying in many cases:

- promotion of their academic subject;
- personal reputation gain within the university;
- personal reputation gain externally, with peers in their academic community;
- wish to promote own teaching materials, such as textbooks and software;
- wish to promote a research project to a wider community (impact, dissemination);
- wish to carry out 'citizen science' with the learners on a MOOC;
- generally interested in educational developments and innovation;
- wish to see how to use MOOCs for enhancement of on-campus (residential teaching);
- wish to see how to use MOOCs for enhancement of taught online education;
- wish to earn income for academic department;
- wish to earn income for self (depending upon remuneration scheme in operation);
- recruited/volunteered by colleagues to join MOOC team (essential skills needed);
- recruited/volunteered by senior manager(s) onto MOOC for strategic reasons.

In broader conversations these reasons seem to be widespread. The reasons why faculty decline to become involved are perhaps harder to uncover, perhaps because for many faculty they prefer to remain silent or absent from discussion about a topic where a negative view might be uncomfortable to hold. In some instances, collective negative views about MOOCs have been expressed by faculty, mainly in the US (CHE, 2013; Kolowich, 2013).

Creating, Delivering, Sustaining and Closing MOOCs

The world of MOOCs is an agile one. The normally slow-paced traditional academic governance and course production processes are not well suited to the rapid pace needed to take maximum advantage of the opportunities offered by MOOCs. At Edinburgh, we found that there were several aspects of entering this world that demanded speed: the decision to enter/refrain from offering MOOCs; the selection of which potential MOOCs to offer (perhaps more importantly which to decline); the MOOC production cycle; and the academic approval processes around curriculum design. Adopting a fast approach entails taking risks, due to lack of time to reflect as fully as might be wished.

Making a decision as to whether to offer MOOCs has demanded speed for several reasons – regular media/press interest in whether or not your university is joining this 'online revolution' that requires a cogent and careful answer; the same questions from Councils/Courts; competitiveness between universities to be in the vanguard, especially when political interest rises; and the need to accept promptly an offer to join a MOOC platform for fear that it may not be repeated if declined, or may not remain on the table if not responded to promptly. This is not to say that speed has to be accepted as the price to pay to be among MOOC providers, but that pressure for speed may well be felt by those in the decision-making seats. At Edinburgh, we made our decision to join Coursera in the early days of the MOOC platforms, in a time period of several days, which puts the process alongside such decisions as unexpected major research grant or building purchase opportunities, and in a different timeframe for that deployed when deciding new courses or degrees. This timeframe may be more familiar for senior academic managers and less familiar to faculty, and sometimes this may be the cause of some disquiet on the part of the latter.

Fast decision-making requires agile governance; offering MOOCs has some of the features needed for successful innovation within organisations as described recently by John Kotter (2012). The key actors need to understand governance well enough to be able to operate it at speed, and at Edinburgh we based our governance for MOOCs on that used to help us manage major non-estate projects by classifying them into strategic, major and minor depending upon their potential impacts, risks and costs. Interestingly, unlike most major projects, including our substantial expansion of taught online Master degree programmes at the University of Edinburgh, the costs of MOOCs are very low in comparison to their potential impacts and their risks. The toolkit we use can be found on the University Projects website.

Our rapid deliberations around whether to offer MOOCs, in partnership with Coursera in early summer 2012 when the company was very small, focussed mainly on reputational risk and exit strategy. Our governance methodology guided us to consult our top level body, University Court (which was strongly supportive), our extended senior management team and our student association. The speed of the process meant that a wider discussion with faculty via academic schools and Senatus was not feasible, and at that stage we were unclear quite what offering MOOCs would mean, at what scale we might expand to and how a return on the investment might be ensured. Because the MOOCs were not credit bearing, we decided on a 'light' course approval process by taking the curricula for the MOOCs to our top level Senatus committee (Curriculum and Student Progression), and at the same time 'educating' them about the nature of MOOCs and their implications. As this committee has the academic leads from the Colleges plus members of the University senior team, this was felt to be sufficient curriculum oversight for what were, in essence, short extension or lifelong learning courses. We agreed to do the same with the quality assurance (QA) process, and take the outcomes of each MOOC (eg data on enrolment and departure, satisfaction with the course) to the top level Senatus committee (Senatus Quality Assurance).

At the present time, and perhaps for some time, the decision to cease offering MOOCs or to leave a particular MOOC platform, especially if it is high profile, will be even harder than joining, and will require particularly careful governance and management. We discovered that even our decision to join Futurelearn while also a partner in Coursera provoked strong media interest, as they tried to work out if we were unhappy with Coursera (we were not, and are not, unhappy) or were hedging our bets on possible differential success of the two platforms (again, this wasn't a reason – we felt they offered us different and complementary affordances in terms of the peer network and audience coverage). The leaving decision is likely to be a relatively slow process in universities and other MOOC platform partners unless forced by a radical change in the MOOC platform.

For the faculty, speed is a key ingredient in getting them on board with offering MOOCs as they want their ideas to reach maturity as quickly as possible, partly through concern that 'someone else will do the same MOOC first', and partly because the faculty who want to create MOOCs are drawn from the pool of innovation leaders who have ideas and drive, in research as well as in teaching. They don't want to be bogged down in red tape and procedure, which would contrast poorly with the excitement of offering short, open courses to the world. Thus selection of MOOCs, rapid agreement on which will be supported and short timescales to development to launch have proved important to us in our MOOC programme at Edinburgh and with colleagues in our peer universities with whom we have talked. This requires strong leadership to control number, quality and funding for MOOC choice and development for the best return to the university, plus a significant commitment of administrative time to manage the 'gateway processes' between the university and the MOOC platforms (legals, copyright clearance, disability compliance). For universities deciding to join more than one MOOC platform, these gateway processes can constitute quite a significant effort, and the additional decision-making around which MOOC is placed on which platform can be quite challenging if faculty disagree with the gatekeepers!

In many respects, the decision to become a MOOC provider is the easy part – living up to the decision, and delivering a portfolio of high quality online courses, is much harder and lasts for a considerable time.

Costs, Benefits and Return on Investment of MOOCs

Throughout 2012 a regular media and press question was: 'What does it cost to develop a MOOC?' (Haywood et al., 2013; Grainger, 2013; Morrison, 2014). This was mirrored by similar queries to us from colleagues in universities which were themselves considering joining a MOOC platform. A rough consensus has emerged among those universities prepared to offer comment on this subject, and that is that a single MOOC costs around US$50k, varying on complexity and duration (they are generally 5–12 weeks long, with mode of 7 weeks (Bayne and Ross, 2014)). That cost may not include start-up activities that often require the establishment of a dedicated video production service (as it did for us in Edinburgh) and also often not the cost of senior staff time (which we have found to be substantial if maximum value is to be extracted, see later). Thus we estimate that a portfolio of approximately thirty MOOCs will require investment of between US$1M and US$2M to create and deliver them over a three-year period. For large research-intensive universities, which were the original entrants into MOOCs, this is a very small percentage of their annual turnover (e.g. for Edinburgh approx. 0.15 per cent), although for universities in less strong financial positions this could be viewed as a significant sum to invest. Clearly, much of the income of these universities is restricted, being research funding, and so we should perhaps approximately double the percentage to reflect disposable income (therefore for Edinburgh 0.3 per cent total, or 0.1 per cent per annum). The great majority of this cost per MOOC comes from faculty time committed to their development and delivery, and so comes from 'sunk costs', although the consequent opportunity cost in faculty time of producing MOOCs did feature in our Edinburgh senior management team's consideration of how many MOOCs to offer (perhaps not in excess of forty), and how to manage the process of selection and development.

The actual and foreseen benefits to us from offering our first six MOOCs have proven to be real and diverse, and in some important respects different to those that we anticipated at the outset (Haywood, Macleod and Woodgate, 2013). Our reasons for joining Coursera have been, or are being, justified and beyond:

- *Reputation*: we have had substantial reputational gain from our first six MOOCs through, for example, one that is very innovative in pedagogy, one that has high 'retention' and two that are being re-used by others. This has not come by being passive and 'letting the MOOCs do the work'. We have been assiduous in speaking to and writing for the media, the press, at conferences and with key leaders in the UK and worldwide, offering consistent messages; that has been demanding for junior and senior colleagues alike.

- *Educational R&D*: into this broad area we can put substantial increases in educational research, expanding our already strong presence; design and testing of an online course for TAs in MOOC support; experimentation with different types of short, focussed video for MOOCs that can be re-used, and even with a video-less MOOC; gains in confidence about how best to use crowd-sourced support and large scale peer review in humanities and social sciences subjects; an understanding of how to create a sense of high faculty 'touch' in MOOCs in the most efficient way; and a different insight into learning analytics and development of the skills and toolset for wider deployment (Knox and Bayne, 2014, Knox et al., 2012, Knox et al., 2014).

- *Increased interest in online learning*: some faculty have switched from being neutral to very interested in online learning as a consequence of their experiences offering, or even thinking about, MOOCs. This interest applies to both taught fully online courses as well as better use of technology in on-campus courses. We had mainly expected that the 'usual suspects', already well ahead with taught online courses, would be the main drivers of MOOCs, and in the early stages that was true, although probably substantially because they were 'targeted' to be our spearhead entrants. This is a very welcome additional benefit, as it aligns with our University intention to expand online education across all levels of the curriculum and all academic subjects towards our 2025 vision.

- *Recruitment*: we have clear evidence that a small (as a fraction of total enrolments) number of individuals have enrolled on Edinburgh postgraduate courses following their positive experiences with our MOOCs, and some less robust evidence that undergraduate applicants are aware and influenced by MOOCs. As the income from student fees is a significant element of the university's budgets this is a welcome development, and even a small additional enrolment can bring important fee income. Other universities have also reported similar outcomes, e.g. University of London International for its distance learning programmes (Grainger, 2013).

- *Outcome agreements*: our national (Scottish) HE funding agency requires statements from universities about what they will do in the coming year in key areas, such as the student experience and widening participation. We have been able to bring our MOOCs into those agreements (SFC, 2014) and in so doing to step beyond the more traditional approaches, including MOOCs for community development and action (e.g. social justice, sustainable energy).

Nevertheless, we are very aware that the return on investment (ROI) for the first six MOOCs may well not hold true for the next twenty or so; as the number of MOOCs and platforms increases, duplication of MOOCs grows, press and media interest wanes and, perhaps, political attention wanders. To get a continuing high ROI, especially on second and subsequent offerings of each MOOC, we shall have to work on (i.e. put cost into) promoting our MOOCs, making them as high quality and innovative as possible, getting interesting stories to the media, and aligning our use of open courses with the national/regional political agenda for higher education. We will lower production costs due to a smoother, better tuned process, but design and production time will always be relatively high given the nature of online learning courses. Colleagues at EPFL in Switzerland call it the 'MOOC Factory' (EPFL, 2014). In many ways, this feels quite far removed from the fun of the early days!

Where Next with MOOCs at the University of Edinburgh?

As of the end of 2013, the University of Edinburgh has seven MOOCs that have been offered at least once (six on Coursera, one on Futurelearn), four that have been offered or used more than once, and twenty-four that are due to be launched before mid-2015. Each will have a minimum lifespan of three years and so, at present, the latest point for us to 'gracefully' cease offering MOOCs would be mid-2018, i.e. six years from the initial decision point to begin offering them.

A clear trend, and perhaps a surprisingly rapid development given the generally slow transition into online learning for many research-intensive universities, has been an exploration by many universities of 'other ways to use MOOCs' – or MOOC-plus as we shall describe it as a convenient shorthand. We are no exception, and have begun to explore opportunities to use our MOOCs in other than the 'standard' way, to use MOOCs from other institutions and to create collaborative, inter-university/organisation MOOCs (Bartholet, 2013).

Moving in this direction has required us to review our governance and management processes for MOOCs to ensure that they are appropriate, and we are planning the road to mainstreaming MOOC creation and deployment into the normal academic processes. This will place decisions about whether to offer a MOOC(s), and the curriculum approval and post hoc QA firmly in the academic School and in the review processes through subject-level Boards of Study to the Senatus committees. Financing MOOCs will also become more devolved, with less central funding and more responsibility to assess the value of the business case within the School. This may have risks that the university-wide benefits of MOOCs may not be sufficient to encourage School-level investment. Central support for video instructional design will remain, although this will move from a 'special forces unit' into the core University technology-enhanced learning team, which will promote better cross-talk between those supporting technology in on-campus, taught online and MOOC courses. Senior management team responsibility will transfer from its current position with the current SMT member (VP/CIO/Librarian) to the Vice Principal (=Provost) for Learning and Teaching. The university will still manage the access to the MOOC platforms and the strategic and operational relationship with them.

There is a real challenge for us in carrying out this mainstreaming; we still need the ability to be agile if particularly important MOOC opportunities arise and we invested more rapidly in MOOCs than we traditionally have in core technology for learning and teaching, so a normalised funding stream to remove barriers to MOOC construction will be required. A recent Senatus meeting for faculty about online learning raised no challenges or adverse reaction to our explorations, giving us confidence that we have our faculty with us in this area of innovation.

So where will MOOCs take us as a university sector? Can we see any trends in early 2014 that might enable us to predict a few years ahead?

It seems likely that the number of MOOC platforms will continue to rise and perhaps, importantly, beyond the Anglophone/Roman character set countries. One MOOC platform has appeared in the Gulf region (*Rwaq* (رواق)) www. rwaq.org/) and it would be surprising not to see others there and in the Indian subcontinent, China and SE Asia. Some of these will emerge from universities, some privately/commercially and some government sponsored/funded (MOOCs.co, 2014). Within the existing platforms recruitment of new university and agency/ organisation partners continues, and so as each offers a portfolio of MOOCs, the total number of MOOCs will continue to rise. The desire of each university and platform to distinguish itself from the others and establish some form of unique selling proposition (USP) will increase diversity in the range of subjects, study levels and pedagogical approaches on offer. We can observe this now in the actions of the existing dominant platforms to offer features such as 'mobile first', 'specialisations' and 'practical and career-oriented subjects'. The search for new audiences will drive platform SMTs to market more intensely and with greater focus, especially if competition from regional and local platforms ramps up. Some platforms may well close, having found no viable business model. They will leave their partners with MOOCs but without a platform, which they may well find uncomfortable, especially if joining another platform proves difficult. Hedging bets by joining more than one platform may become the order of the day.

For universities not currently offering MOOCs, the expansion of platforms offers a chance to enter the field, albeit for those that join existing markets, with limited expectations for enrolments and global brand enhancement. By contrast, they may take a different approach, and look to operate with lower costs and target more local markets, and be more focussed on recruitment into fee-bearing courses than the early wave of entrants.

One thing is certain, MOOCs will be here for several years to come. Their impact on the way that we in higher education, and perhaps those in policy and government circles, think about the way that university education can be designed and delivered will have changed. We should work to ensure that the changes are for the better.

References

Bartholet, J. (2013) Free Online Courses Bring 'Magic' to Rwanda. *Scientific American* 309 (2): www.scientificamerican.com/article/free-online-classes-bring-magic-rwanda/ (accessed 22 January 2014).

Bayne, S. and Ross, J. (2014) *The Pedagogy of the Massive Open Online Course (MOOC): The UK View*. Higher Education Academy: www.heacademy.ac.uk/resources/detail/ elt/the_pedagogy_of_the_MOOC_UK_view (accessed 22 January 2014).

CHE (2013) San Jose State U's Faculty Association Responds to the MOOC Backlash, *Chronicle of Higher Education* 9 May: http://chronicle.com/article/Document-San-Jose-State-Us/139139/ (accessed 22 January 2014).

EPFL (2014) MOOCs Factory, Centre for Digital Education, Ecole Polytechnique Federale de Lausanne: http://moocs.epfl.ch/mooc-factory (accessed 22 January 2014).

Grainger, B. (2013) MOOC Report 2013, University of London International Programmes: www.londoninternational.ac.uk/sites/default/files/documents/mooc_report-2013.pdf (accessed 22 January 2014).

Haywood, J. (2012) No Such Thing as a Free MOOC: www.jisc.ac.uk/blog/no-such-thing-as-a-free-mooc-20-jul-2012 (accessed 22 January 2014).

Haywood, J., Macleod, H.A. and Woodgate, A. (2013) *MOOCs @ Edinburgh 2013—Report #1*: www.era.lib.ed.ac.uk/handle/1842/6683 (accessed 22 January 2014).

Knox, J. and Bayne, S. (2014) Multimodal Profusion in the Literacies of the Massive Open Online Course. *Research in Learning Technology*, 21: 21422 – http://dx.doi.org/10.3402/rlt.v21.21422 (accessed 22 January 2014).

Knox, J., Bayne, S., Macleod, H., Ross, J. and Sinclair, C. (2012) MOOC Pedagogy: The Challenges of Developing for Coursera. *ALT Online Newsletter.* https://newsletter.alt.ac.uk/2012/08/mooc-pedagogy-the-challenges-of-developing-for-coursera/ (accessed 22 January 2014).

Knox, J., Ross, J., Sinclair, C., Macleod, H., and Bayne, S. (2014) MOOC Feedback: pleasing all the people?. In S. Krause and C. Lowe, *Invasion of the MOOC*. Anderson, SC: Parlor Press: www.parlorpress.com/invasion_of_the_moocs (accessed 22 January 2014).

Kolowich, S. (2013) Harvard Professors Call for Greater Oversight of MOOCs, *Chronicle of Higher Education* 24 May: http://chronicle.com/blogs/wiredcampus/harvard-professors-call-for-greater-oversight-of-moocs/43953 (accessed 22 January 2014).

Kotter, J. P. (2012) *Leading Change*. Boston, MA: Harvard Business Review Press.

MOOCs.co (2014) A comprehensive list of platforms and national initatives can be found on the *Global Directory of MOOC providers by market segment* website: Higher Education MOOCs, www.moocs.co/Higher_Education_MOOCs.html (accessed 22 January 2014); Further Education and other level MOOCs, www.moocs.co/Other_MOOCs.html (accessed 22 January 2014).

Morrison, D. (2014) How and Why Institutions are Engaging with MOOCs . . . Answers in Report 'MOOCs: Expectations and Reality': https://onlinelearninginsights.word press.com/tag/costs-of-developing-a-mooc/ (accessed 22 January 2014).

Parr, C. (2013) If You Want to Make it with Moocs, You Must Stand Out from the Crowd: www.timeshighereducation.co.uk/if-you-want-to-make-it-with-moocs-you-must-stand-out-from-the-crowd/422234.article (accessed 22 January 2014).

Parr, C. (2014) Interview for *Times Higher Education* with Sir Timothy O'Shea, University of Edinburgh: www.timeshighereducation.co.uk/comment/podcasts/the-podcast-sir-tim-oshea-interview/2012383.article (accessed 22 January 2014).

SFC (2014) Outcomes Agreement with University of Edinburgh, Scottish Higher Education Funding Council pp. 9, 12 and 16: www.sfc.ac.uk/web/FILES/Funding_Outcome_Agreements_2014–15/University_of_Edinburgh_Outcome_Agreement_2014–17.pdf (accessed 22 January 2014).

Straumsheim, C. (2013) Scaling Back in San Jose, *Inside Higher Ed*, 18 December: www.insidehighered.com/news/2013/12/18/san-jose-state-u-resurrects-scaled-back-online-course-experiment-mooc-provider#sthash.2K3m5nK8.L2St4cMJ.dpbs (accessed 22 January 2014).

4

ENTER THE ANTI-MOOCS

The Reinvention of Online Learning as a Form of Social Commentary

Larry Johnson and Samantha Adams Becker

Introduction

The term "massive open online course," (MOOC) although coined in 2008 by Stephen Downes and George Siemens, really came into broad use in 2012. Since then, MOOCs have gained public awareness with a ferocity not seen in some time. World-renowned universities, including MIT and Harvard University (edX) and Stanford University (Coursera), as well as innovative start-ups such as Udacity, jumped into the marketplace with huge splashes, and have garnered a tremendous amount of attention—and imitation. Designed to provide high quality online learning at scale to people regardless of their location or educational background, MOOCs have been met with enthusiasm because of their potential to reach a previously unimaginable number of learners. The notion of thousands and even tens of thousands of students participating in a single course—working at their own pace, relying on their own style of learning, and assessing each other's progress—has changed the landscape of online learning.

A number of respected thought leaders, however, believe that the current manifestation of MOOCs has significantly deviated from the initial premise outlined by George Siemens and Stephen Downes when they pioneered the first courses in Canada. They envisioned MOOCs as ecosystems of connectivism— a pedagogy in which knowledge is not a destination but an ongoing activity, fueled by the relationships people build and the deep discussions catalyzed within the MOOC. That model emphasizes knowledge production over consumption, and new knowledge that emerges from the process helps to sustain and evolve the MOOC environment.

While extremely promising, the more current MOOC models differ from those connectivist models, and largely mirror traditional lecture formats. Coursera, for example, is centered around video lectures led by renowned educators from prestigious universities in popular areas such as microeconomics and artificial intelligence. Students watch these videos and demonstrate what they have learned via quizzes and papers. Although the quality of the video and related content provided is high, this delivery model is very much based on traditional models of instruction, and does not include the notions of openness and connectivism outlined by Siemens and Downes. Indeed, the content on each of the major sites is not "open," as pervasive copyright notices make clear.

Coursera, edX, and Udacity, the three major players in the MOOC space, have put a lot of money and effort into developing high quality proprietary content, which is housed in learning environments that each bring their own unique and proprietary "secret sauce." A variety of forms of machine intelligence have been developed as part of these systems to assess student performance. The social structures of the major MOOC projects are essentially similar, with students participating in online forums, study groups, and in the case of Coursera and Udacity, organized student meet-ups. Content-wise, Coursera emphasizes video, with students watching recorded lectures from field experts as the main substance of the courses. At the time of publication, Coursera had over four million students enrolled in 400 courses, while edX and Udacity had reached 1.75 million students, across 60 courses and 30 courses, respectively.

In response to what many see as problems in the pedagogical, financial, and other models of the high profile MOOC providers, a curious form of social commentary has emerged—the "Anti-MOOC," a term coined by Audrey Watters that refers to online courses that are specifically positioned as experiments in online learning that, in well-defined ways, do not ascribe to the models used by the Courseras, Udacities, and other large providers.

Anti-MOOCs have a unique role as counterpoint to the more high-profile online learning projects. As massive open online courses continue their high-speed trajectory, many educational leaders and theorists feel that there is a great need for reflection—especially that which includes frank discussions about what a sustainable, successful model looks like. In this context, many Anti-MOOCs are high-level experiments in online learning created expressly to generate a counterpoint to MOOCs and a basis for social interaction and commentary.

In some ways, this may reflect the view of many experts that the pace at which MOOCs are developing is too rapid for genuine analysis; alternatives need to be created to provide comparison points. Others maintain that MOOCs are not the disruptive technology initially touted, and that the current landscape is uniquely (and probably only temporarily) open to new ideas in online learning.

When MOOCs were Young

When Stephen Downes and George Siemens coined the term in 2008, massive open online courses were conceptualized as the next evolution of networked learning. The essence of the original MOOC concept was a web course that people could take from anywhere across the world, with potentially thousands of participants. The basis of this concept is an expansive and diverse set of content, contributed by a variety of experts, educators, and instructors in a specific field, and aggregated into a central repository, such as a website. What made this content set especially unique is that it could be "remixed"—the materials were not necessarily designed to go together but became associated with each other through the MOOC. A key component of the original vision is that all course materials and the course itself were open source and free—with the door left open for a fee if a participant taking the course wanted university credit to be transcripted for the work.

Except for a few notable exceptions, such as the compelling DS106 from the University of Mary Washington (UMW), this constructivist model has not found much traction among MOOC designers. Early MOOCs leveraged a multitude of established and emerging pedagogies and tools, including blended learning, open educational resources, and crowd-sourced interaction. The technologies that enable the workflow of early MOOCs varied, but the common thread has been that these sorts of tools were readily available and easy to use. The first MOOCs drew upon cloud-based services such as WikiSpaces, YouTube, and Google Hangouts, among many others, to foster discussions, create and share videos, and engage in all the other activities that over the last five years or so have become essential to teaching and learning in a modern online learning environment.

While the influence of these early MOOCs on online pedagogy has been significant, it is important to remember that online learning is not new. The category encompasses any learning that takes place through web-based platforms, whether formal or informal, and online learning providers have been toiling in these fields for more than 20 years. What has made the topic new is the recent and unprecedented focus on providing learning via the Internet that has been stimulated by the tremendous interest in massive open online courses.

MOOCs received their fair share of hype as they exploded onto the education landscape in 2012. Big name providers including Coursera, edX, and Udacity count hundreds of thousands of enrolled students, totals that when added together illustrate their popularity. One of the most appealing promises of MOOCs is that they offer the possibility for continued, advanced learning at zero cost, allowing students, life-long learners, and professionals to acquire new skills and improve their knowledge and employability all of the time. MOOCs have enjoyed one of the fastest uptakes ever seen in higher education. Yet critics loudly warn that there is a need to examine these new approaches through a critical lens to ensure they are effective and evolve past the traditional lecture-style pedagogies.

MOOCs as Big Business

In 2012, the Federal Reserve Bank of New York reported that Americans owe over $900 billion in student loans. At the same time, 40 percent of university students across the nation do not complete a degree within 6 years. There is a growing number of students concerned about what they are actually getting in exchange for the tremendous costs of their education. As inexorably as Moore's Law has governed the shrinking size of transistors and chips, higher education budgets seem to be following a sort of inverse of the law, in which costs rise year upon year, with tuition rates rising even faster as public support dwindles.

This is the environment in which MOOCs have prospered. More than any idea that has come along in years, university presidents and boards of trustees see a new business model in these large-scale courses, and as such have invested a great deal of efforts in exploring their potential. In October 2012, Stanford University President John Hennessy referred to the incredible pace of development in MOOCs as a tsunami. "I can't tell you exactly how it's going to break, but my goal is to try to surf it, not to just stand there," he said in a panel discussion on the changing economics of education.

The major players are all well known: Coursera, started by two computer science professors at Stanford University; Udacity, which emerged from a Stanford University experiment in which Sebastian Thrun and Peter Norvig put their class on artificial intelligence online, with tremendous results; and edX, the lone nonprofit based in Cambridge, Massachusetts that was founded and is jointly governed by MIT and Harvard. Each has invested millions in their own online learning platforms. The main difference between them is the courses they have to offer and the structure and style of delivery of these courses.

Coursera was founded in 2011 and publicly launched its proprietary platform in April 2012. More than 80 institutions, including Yale, Northwestern, and Stanford, offer some 400 courses. The company claimed more than four million students in late 2013. Among the major players, Coursera has generated the most funding, with more than $65 million invested so far. In January 2013, the company launched a new service that it said could be its biggest source of revenue: selling "verified certificates" that authenticate students' identities and offer a more valuable credential. Titled "Signature Track," the new program garnered 25,000 signups and earned $1 million in revenue by September 2013.

Udacity, founded in 2012, famously began as a hugely successful experiment by Stanford University professors, Sebastian Thrun and Peter Norvig, who put their class on artificial intelligence online. Thrun is the inventor of Google's self-driving car and one of the forces behind Google Glass. Unlike edX and Coursera, Udacity produces courses in its own studio, rather than distributing content created by universities; their 30 courses are taught by faculty from at least 5 universities, plus private partner companies such as Google, NVIDIA, Microsoft, and Autodesk. As of the end of 2012, the company reported more than 750,000 students. Udacity raised $21.1 million in capital by December 2012, and the number of courses doubled in 2013, with high-profile partnerships announced with the Georgia Institute of Technology (Georgia Tech) and San Jose State.

However, the company has experienced challenges in 2013; in January, San Jose State was signed as a major partner, with a major for-credit course experiment planned, but early results were mixed, and in July, the effort was put on hold. Georgia Tech is currently working with Udacity in an online master's degree that gives students a real economic incentive.

Georgia Tech's master's degree in computer science was launched in January 2014 using Udacity's platform and they are currently charging students only $6,700, far less than the $45,000 that the same program would cost on campus. This initiative is certainly a pioneering approach for an elite institution. If it approaches its goal of drawing thousands of students, it will signal a profound change to the landscape of higher education in years to come.

edX, the sole not-for-profit entity in the top 3, was founded in May 2012, and has grown to include 28 institutions in what is called the xConsortium. The organization offers about 60 courses on its open source platform, and claimed 1 million registered users in June 2013. Led by co-founders MIT and Harvard, plus Berkeley and Cornell, edX has $60 million in funding from Harvard and MIT in startup money, along with another $1 million from the Bill and Melinda Gates Foundation. In February 2–13 and then again in May, edX doubled its university partners and expanded abroad.

The early success of the major players, and the tremendous attention they have drawn, both in terms of student interest and funding, created a firestorm in both the educational and financial press. By the end of 2012, MOOCs were the topic of discussions at the highest levels at virtually every major university.

With the tremendous focus and attention on the phenomenon, inevitably the hype began to build. Traditional universities were doomed, so the conventional wisdom went, condemned to irrelevance by an onslaught of MOOCs. According to *Wired*, in early 2012, Udacity's Sebastian Thrun mused that 10 might survive.

MOOCs in Transition

Barely a year later, the tide has turned. What education experts and journalists once lauded as innovative and exciting has now become the subject of criticism in a stream of news stories and blogs that questioned how far apart the promise and reality have been. After a year of hype and curiosity, concrete data on the results of the early MOOC offerings finally surfaced, and the results have added fuel to the critical fire.

Even Sebastian Thrun, Udacity's founder, has adopted a new perspective based on the initial findings. In a comment to *The Chronicle of Higher Education*, he said, "A medium where only self-motivated, web-savvy people sign up, and the success rate is 10% doesn't strike me quite yet as a solution to the problems of higher education" (see Kolowich 2013a).

Thrun's shift in stance is significant, and signals a new view of MOOCs that is more critical and less willing to be supportive of MOOCs in general. As Jonathan Rees (2013) quipped on his *More or Less Bunk* blog, "Anti-MOOC really is the new black."

In July 2013, the end of San Jose's State University's high profile MOOCs-for-credit experiment with Udacity after just six months marked the turning point for many. The pendulum of public fascination began to swing back with a vengeance, and an outpouring of articles and commentaries suggested that MOOCs, far from being the "single most important experiment in higher education," as *The Atlantic* put it in July 2012, are increasingly under a very critical microscope. That same month, George Siemens (2013) observed on his *ELEARNSPACE* blog that, "Critiquing MOOCs is now more fashionable than advocating for them."

Some thought leaders, on the other hand, view the initial disappointing data spawned by MOOCs as unsurprising, and symptomatic of higher education in general. Jonathan Tapson detailed these viewpoints as falling into two rather succinct perspectives: many advocates of the status quo argue that a high-quality student–teacher or student–peer interaction is all but impossible on the web, while others, pointing to very low completion rates with MOOCs (from 5 to 16 percent), argue that they are *ipso facto* not effective substitutes for real education.

Tapson (2013) counters this last point, by noting that "a small percentage of a very large number is still a large number. When 14% of the 160,000 students who signed up for Udacity's Introduction to Programming passed, that added up to 23,000 completions." He went on to observe that across the four universities in which he had worked, this common freshman course probably had fewer than 10,000 completions in those institutions' entire histories. Udacity managed this in three months, he observed, with a staff of less than a dozen, and on a budget far less than the sum those four university departments probably spent on it combined.

Others, including Doug Guthrie (2013) at *Forbes*, are very concerned about the ongoing revelations of poor test results, high dropout rates, and disgruntled university instructors. He partly attributes these outcomes to a lack of innovation in higher education pedagogy and, from that perspective, thinks it is clear that MOOCs are not the panacea for twenty-first-century higher education that their proponents claimed they would be. "MOOCs have turned out to be only a minor achievement in pedagogy," he noted, "and an expensive one at that." In Guthrie's view, MOOCs were largely online lecture halls, yet "nobody in the business of instructional design feels that lecture halls, whether on campus or online are a good way to teach students."

Not all the news is critical. As Tamar Lewin of *The New York Times* wrote, since the first free artificial intelligence course from Stanford enrolled 170,000 students 2 years ago, MOOCs have drawn millions of people to sample learning from the world's top universities. There have been heartwarming results, such as the perfect scores of Battushig, a 15-year-old Mongolian boy, in a rigorous electronics course offered by MIT.

Nonetheless, as Lewin goes on to note, while there is justifiable excitement around the reach of these courses, MOOCs have not delivered on the expectation of profound change in his view because they offer no credit and do not lead to a degree. Levin feels that the decision of Georgia Tech to offer a MOOC-based online master's degree in computer science for $6,600 could be a game-changer. The dean of the Georgia Tech's College of Computing, Zvi Galil, expects that the program could attract up to 10,000 students. Notably, the program may be a response to declining international enrollments as well. "Online, there's no visa problem," he said in Lewin's *The New York Times* article (2013).

The prospect of a low-cost degree from a world-class institution has generated tremendous interest. Some, Lewin (2013) writes, think the leap from individual non-credit courses to full degree programs could signal the next phase in the evolution of MOOCs and bring real change to higher education. While some believe in the potential of MOOCs and others see the movement as all hype, there is a middle ground; the fact that the topic is being discussed so intensely means that it has opened the doors to new ideas. MOOCs have catalyzed countless conversations about how to improve online learning—what is working and what is not.

"Perhaps Zvi Galil and Sebastian Thrun will prove to be the Wright brothers of MOOCs," said S. James Gates Jr., a University of Maryland physicist who serves on President Obama's Council of Advisors on Science and Technology.

> This is the first deliberate and thoughtful attempt to apply education technology to bringing instruction to scale. It could be epoch-making. If it really works, it could begin the process of lowering the cost of education, and lowering barriers for millions of Americans.
>
> (Gates Jr., see Lewin 2013)

Even for those who recognize vast potential in MOOCs, it is still challenging to discern what will happen next and which efforts will be successful. Georgia Tech's Dr. Galil is primarily concerned with breaking new ground.

"This is all uncharted territory, so no one really knows if it will go to scale," Dr. Galil said. "We just want to prove that it can be done, to make a high-quality degree program available for a low cost." In response, Lewin asked, "Would such a program cannibalize campus enrollment?" (Lewin 2013).

"Frankly, nobody knows," answered Galil, and it is still far from certain if the degree program will be sustainable. While a single pilot effort may be successful, expanding to include more for-credit MOOCs across institutional offerings poses its own set of problems, requiring a larger financial investment for more instructional design, scaffolding, and staff. Some are skeptical that tuition for fee-based MOOCs can remain as low as they are in the Georgia Tech model.

"The whole MOOC mania has got everyone buzzing in academia, but scaling is a great challenge," said Bruce Chaloux, who until his recent untimely death was executive director of the Sloan Consortium, an advocacy group for online education. "I have to believe that at some point, when the underwriting ends, to keep high quality, Georgia Tech would have to float to more traditional tuition rates" (see Lewin 2013).

Even if providers find ways for the costs of for-credit MOOCs to remain modest, there is still the lingering question of whether the degrees will ever be valued as highly as those from brick-and-mortar institutions—or at all.

"Georgia Tech is exceptionally important because it's a prestigious institution offering an important degree at very low cost with a direct connection to a Fortune 100 corporation that will use it to fill their pipeline," said Terry W. Hartle, the senior vice president of the American Council on Education. "It addresses a lot of the issues about universities that the public cares about. But how good and how transferable it is remains to be seen" (see Lewin 2013).

Students on MOOCs

For students, the promise of MOOCs is very appealing at the surface. Many current models present opportunities for learners to freely experiment with a variety of subjects and acquire new skills that may not be associated with a degree plan at brick-and-mortar institutions. An English major, for example, could enroll in an edX course on the foundations of computer graphics or circuits and electronics.

One such student, 21-year-old Feynman Liang, has completed 36 massive open online courses through Udacity and Coursera—while simultaneously pursuing majors at both Amherst College and Dartmouth University. He believes the combination of face-to-face and online courses have given him a more well-rounded education. "A big reason why I'm able to have taken so many MOOCs is because I'm fortunate to be in an environment which enables it," Liang (2013) reported to TheGoodMOOC.com. "Professors and other students provide me with an intellectual community I can go to whenever I have questions about things being covered in MOOCs."

At the same time, Liang notes a concern. "I find MOOCs to particularly excel when it comes to lectures and assignments requiring little creativity," said Liang. "Traditional classrooms are superior to MOOCs when it comes to personalized mentoring and uniform standards, which make assigning creative assignments particularly difficult."

While Liang does not believe that the quality of MOOCs will surpass that of traditional, face-to-face learning experiences, he recognizes their promise. "By shifting the lecture and homework part of the classroom to an online platform, professors can focus on adding value through personalized mentoring and open-ended projects."

Liang's balanced perspective is an important part of the ongoing conversation around MOOCs, and points to a future in which MOOCs have an understood and valuable role to play in concert with more formal education approaches. Others see a need to move to new models, informed by the MOOC experiments, but which include other elements, including more personalization and interactivity, along with improved engagement strategies.

Enter the Anti-MOOCs

In this mix, some institutions are calling for an end to MOOC mania, and making impassioned arguments for more measured approaches. The administration at American University has issued a "moratorium on MOOCs," according to *The Chronicle of Higher Education*. "America is purposely avoiding experimentation before it decides exactly how it wants to relate to the new breed of online courses. I need a policy before we jump into something," said Scott A. Bass, the provost, in an interview (Kolowich 2013b).

Larry Cuban, in an article for the *Washington Post*, noted that MOOCs have attracted advocates, of course, but also a growing number of skeptics and agnostics, and these two groups are fueling the anti-MOOCs response in a variety of ways. Skeptics, for example, include those who question the premise of learning online as opposed to face-to-face in lecture halls and seminars. Cuban references a recent poll in which nearly 60 percent expressed "more fear than excitement" for expanding online courses. Some of the more active skeptics are urging faculties to take action, lest computer screens replace professors.

Agnostics, Cuban argues, question the hype of MOOCs revolutionizing higher education while seeing both pluses and minuses to virtual learning. They know that approaches such as offering lectures to hundreds of undergraduates are themselves cost-saving strategies. Hybrid teaching practices might indeed be pedagogically superior to large lectures.

Respected blogger Audrey Watters, who may be considered part skeptic and part agnostic on this point, coined the term "Anti-MOOC" in a post about a consortium of ten universities. The group announced a program offering online, for-credit courses in which any students at their respective schools could enroll. Called "Semester Online," the program includes Brandeis University, Duke University, Emory University, Northwestern University, University of North Carolina at Chapel Hill, University of Notre Dame, University of Rochester, Vanderbilt University, Wake Forest University, and Washington University in St. Louis. In this case, the "anti" was aimed at the notion of massiveness—enrollments would be capped at around 20 per course section, a direct rejection of one of the pillars of the large-scale offerings. The University of Maine at Presque Isle is another institution attempting this kind of anti-MOOC approach: a free online offering that is more like the "high-touch" experience of a conventional online course, which Michael Sonntag, the provost, calls a "LOOC"—a "little" open online course.

A partnership between the New Media Consortium (NMC), ISTE, and Hewlett Packard is packaging anti-MOOCs into a comprehensive strategy to deliver professional development to science, engineering, and mathematics teachers at the HP Catalyst Academy. While still building a model that is intended to scale, their notion is to focus primarily on pedagogical innovation, using the medium itself to help deliver the learning. A course on social media, for example, is conducted entirely on Facebook.

Probably the definitive anti-MOOC can be found in Digital Storytelling 106, a very popular online course better known as "DS106." The online digital story-telling course at UMW is one of the few that adheres to the original connectivist notion of a massive online course, open to all, but one must be a registered student at the university to receive credit. Their course also differs from the current MOOC scene because there is no one assigned faculty member to teach it. For the past several years, DS106 has also been taught at several other institutions, and UMW is currently exploring how to give credit to other state college students as well as incoming high school students.

Responses such as these are explicitly citing how what they intend to do is not what MOOCs do—and that is the essence of the anti-MOOC.

One of the founders of the MOOC movement, George Siemens (2013), shared recently on his *ELEARNSPACE* blog, with some cynicism, "If 2012 was the year of the MOOC, 2013 will be the year of the anti-MOOC." Siemens feels that, by and large, faculty do not like MOOCs, and details reasons such as elite university models, poor pedagogy, and blindness to decades of learning sciences research.

Whither, From Here?

Wherever one stands on MOOCs, one thing is clear: online learning has "come of age." The vast scope of articles in the recent press, and even the focus of most research into online learning in the past two years has been on the MOOC phenomenon. Authors and researchers are no longer asking if online learning is effective. We know it can be if well-constructed. More and more, the design of online learning is specifically intended to encompass the latest research, the most promising developments, and new emerging business models in the online learning environment. At many institutions, online learning is an area newly ripe for experimentation—some would argue it is undergoing a sea change, with every dimension of the process open for reconceptualization. On campuses around the globe, virtually every aspect of how students connect with institutions and each other to learn online is being reworked, rethought, and redone—but it will be some time yet before ideas coalesce enough to be validated by research and implemented broadly.

In many current models, massive open online courses present opportunities for learners to freely experiment with a variety of subjects and acquire new skills that may not be associated with a degree plan at brick-and-mortar institutions. A Neurology major, for example, could enroll in a Udacity course on artificial intelligence. Learners are not stuck on a single pathway.

Related advances in both classroom and online learning are emphasizing personalized learning, and if massive open online courses could both scale globally and yet cater to individual learning styles, it would be a very exciting combination. In their current forms, MOOCs already allow learners of all ages, incomes, and levels of education to participate in a wide array of courses without being enrolled at a physical institution. The most effective MOOCs make creative use of a variety of educational strategies and frequently leverage multimedia to demonstrate complex subjects. One recent entrant in Spain, unX, has integrated badges as a way to reward learners for their participation and concept mastery.

If MOOC projects proliferate, advocates hope that providers will invent innovative ways for learners to demonstrate their knowledge at scale. Peer review systems, student gurus, badges, and other forms of assessment are currently being explored, but there is no real verdict yet on what is most effective. To continue to gain traction, MOOCs will need to strike a fine balance between automating the assessment process while delivering personalized, authentic learning opportunities.

It is that last point that brought *Forbes'* Guthrie to suggest that MOOCs are nowhere near the kind of transformative innovation that will remake academia. That honor, according to Guthrie, belongs to a more disruptive and far-reaching innovation—big data and its applications. Big data, he feels, is very likely to revolutionize online learning. It will be the means by which we customize learning to match the needs of individual students, especially in the online learning space. Big data will give institutions the predictive tools they need to improve learning outcomes for individual students. By designing curricula that collect and interpret data at every step of the learning process, customized modules, assignments, and feedback can be targeted to student needs in the moment.

Time and other authors will settle those questions, but there is no doubt that MOOCs have already had a significant influence on the future course of online learning, and continue to do so. Whether it be through the offerings of the large-scale providers, or via the anti-MOOC-inspired online courses at individual universities or consortia, online learning has earned its place in the academy.

Welcome to the new era of online learning!

Online Learning in Practice

A few samples of massive open online courses highlighted in recent Horizon Project research includes the following:

- Acamica is a platform used by Latin American learners to access interactive courses from experts in different areas. As students progress, they build ne knowledge profiles to share with prospective employers or institutions: go.nmc.org/aca.

- Bossier Parish Community College offers an online degree program in which students can do a majority or all of their coursework online. The online instruction involves presentations, video tutorials, discussion boards, and other learning activities: go.nmc.org/bpc.
- The Buena Vista School District launched the Buena Vista Online Academy, an online alternative to a brick-and-mortar school for students: go.nmc.org/bvsdoa.
- Bunker Hill and MassBay Community College partnered with MIT's edX to offer MOOCs to their students. They are the first two-year colleges to work with the popular MOOC provider: go.nmc.org/edXMA.
- The California Institute of Technology piloted the "Learning from Data" MOOC in April 2012. The first offering included live streaming and real-time Q&A sessions with the participants, along with automated grading and discussion forums. Since then it has been offered four times, with over 100,000 enrolled students: go.nmc.org/caltech.
- Colorado Technical College developed an online learning platform called MUSE (My Unique Student Experience), which caters to students' varying learning styles: go.nmc.org/muse.
- The Games MOOC is a community site woven around a series of three courses about the use of games in education, including traditional games, massively multiplayer online role-playing games, game-based learning, and immersive environments. The first courses were piloted in the fall of 2012: go.nmc.org/gamesmooc.
- The Gates Foundation awarded a grant to Ohio State University (OSU) to design a MOOC for Coursera. This course will engage participants as writers, reviewers, and editors in a series of interactive reading, composing, and research activities with assignments designed to help them become more effective consumers and producers of alphabetic, visual, and multimodal texts. OSU faculty members have developed the Writers Exchange, an idea-networking website to support the course: go.nmc.org/osu.
- Google created an open course builder and its first massive open online course, "Power Searching with Google." It drew 150,000 students, and helped sharpen their Internet search skills: go.nmc.org/googco.
- In the spring of 2013, Indiana University-Purdue University Indianapolis and the Purdue University Department of Music and Arts Technology will offer a new MOOC, "Music for the Listener," that can be converted into credit. The six-week course covers the music of western civilization from 600 AD to the present. The learning environment is being delivered through Course Networking, with full translation features, rich media, and social networking tools: go.nmc.org/thecn.

- Maricopa Community Colleges' Career and Technical Education 230: Instructional Technology course stems from a National Science Foundation-funded project to increase the ability of STEM teachers to collaboratively learn and apply STEM skills using information and communication technology. Participating educators acquire knowledge and skills using Canvas and 3D Game Lab learning management systems, and Google+ Community: go.nmc.org/opecou.

- Maricopa Community College offers 600 online courses via a cohort of 10 community colleges, and serves nearly 70,000 students each year: go.nmc.org/maricopa.

- A MOOC called "Landmarks in Physics" delivered through Udacity was created by an MIT graduate who filmed in Italy, the Netherlands, and England to create a virtual tour that explains the basic concepts of physics at the sites of important discoveries in our history: go.nmc.org/phy.

- The online learning platform Veduca provides Brazilian users with 5,000 online classes, licensed from some of the world's top universities, such as MIT, Harvard, Yale, and Princeton, and translates them into Portuguese: go.nmc.org/ved.

- Open Universities Australia launched Australia's first MOOC provider, called Open2Study, in March, 2013: go.nmc.org/ouamooc.

- Senior academic leaders at the University of Queensland have resolved to develop up to twelve open online learning courses over the next two years. Their main interest is in how MOOCs will enable new opportunities for campus-based students: go.nmc.org/uqmooc.

- Oregon Virtual Education is an online learning program that offers free enrollment. Classes can be taken to supplement or replace traditional classroom learning: go.nmc.org/orved.

- Through the open source platform unX, Iberoamerican universities can offer MOOCs for online learning and vocational training. The model includes interactive features, along with a digital badging system: go.nmc.org/unXIA.

- The University of Melbourne became the first Australian university to join Coursera, a leading international online course provider. Macroeconomics and Epigenetics are two of the courses planned to go live by the end of 2013: go.nmc.org/auscou.

- The University of Texas Online High School provides students with an opportunity to receive their high school diplomas through a flexible, distance education model: go.nmc.org/uths.

Further Reading

A sampling of recommended readings related to massively open online courses that have been highlighted in recent Horizon Project research includes the following:

Adaptability to Online Learning: Differences Across Types of Students and Academic Subject Areas

go.nmc.org/adapt
(Di Xu, Community College Research Center, February 2013.) A comparison study examines student success in an online environment.

Colleges Adapt Online Courses to Ease Burden

go.nmc.org/ease
(Tamar Lewin, *The New York Times*, April 29, 2013.) Nearly half of all undergraduates in the US arrive on campus needing more work before they can begin regular classes for credit. Colleges are beginning to experiment with online versions, which allow students to take these initial courses easily and cheaply.

College is Dead. Long Live College!

go.nmc.org/ylazv
(Amanda Ripley, *TIME*, October 18, 2012.) When the Pakistani government shut down access to YouTube, an 11-year-old girl continued her online studies using Udacity.

Credit for MOOCs Presents Challenges in Australia

go.nmc.org/credmo
(Charis Palmer, *The Conversation*, November 7, 2012.) Following the news that Antioch University was working with Coursera to offer credit towards a degree, Australian tertiary education providers debate the possible negative consequences of this approach.

How Online Learning is Saving and Improving Rural High Schools

go.nmc.org/rural
(Tom Vander Ark, *Getting Smart*, January 26, 2013.) Rural high schools face immense challenges, including federal and state education funding inequities, which cause thousands of schools to close down per year. Online schools even the playing field.

How 'Open' Are MOOCs?

go.nmc.org/ope
(Steve Kolowich, *Inside Higher Ed*, November 8, 2012.) This article explores several misunderstandings in the way many chief academic officers view massively open online courses and their potential to supplement traditional university classes.

Jump Off the Coursera Bandwagon

go.nmc.org/cou

(Doug Guthrie, *The Chronicle of Higher Education*, December 17, 2012.) This author observes that as universities rush to deliver online education, they may be too quick to launch insufficient models. As a result, many MOOCs are not addressing critical pedagogical issues, in addition to interactivity and customization.

MOOCs and Money

go.nmc.org/money

(Matt Greenfield, *Education Week*, October 1, 2012.) MOOCs have some possible monetizing strategies that can work as long as they continue to attract millions of students. The author argues that many current students are attracted to MOOCs out of curiosity, and ponders whether enrollment numbers will continue to be high over the next few years.

The Single Most Important Experiment in Higher Education

go.nmc.org/single

(Jordan Weissmann, *The Atlantic*, July 18, 2012) This article discusses Coursera's new partnerships with several other universities. One school, the University of Washington, is giving credit for its Coursera courses. The funding from all these new universities will allow the company to blossom as a market for learning.

States, Districts Require Online Ed for High School Graduation

go.nmc.org/require

(Kelsey Sheehy, *US News*, October 24, 2012.) A growing number of school districts, including those in Virginia and Idaho, have recently signed legislation making it mandatory for students to take at least one online course in order to graduate high school.

The Teacher You've Never Met: Inside an Online High School Class

go.nmc.org/onlinete

(Nick Pandolfo, *TIME*, June 13, 2012.) This article explores the life and work of an online K-12 teacher at Colorado's 21st Century Virtual Academy. The teacher reports frustrations in not being able to read students' body language to better understand their learning needs.

xED Book

go.nmc.org/xed
(Dave Cormier, George Siemens, and Bonnie Stewart, accessed January 2, 2013.)
George Siemens and two education researchers are writing a book that will discuss
how the Internet is restructuring knowledge and the implications for MOOCs.
They are currently chronicling their ideas on this site.

The Year of the MOOC

go.nmc.org/moo
(Laura Pappano, *The New York Times*, November 2, 2012.) Over the past year,
MOOC development has become a major trend. This article examines the current
higher education institutions and organizations offering MOOCs, discussing their
strategies and the challenges each are facing.

References and Suggested Reading

Articles, blog posts, research, and news reports not already cited in the text that were
referenced or used in this paper came from the following sources:

Aders, G. (2013). *Forbes*. "Coursera Hits 4 Million Students—And Triples its Funding."
    From the Internet: www.forbes.com/sites/georgeanders/2013/07/10/coursera-hits-4-
    million-students-and-triples-its-funding/
Cuban, L. (2012). MOOCs and Hype Again. From the Internet: http://larrycuban.word
    press.com/2012/11/21/moocs-and-hype-again/
Guthrie, D. (2013). *Forbes*. "MOOCs are Toast, or at Least Should Be." From the Internet:
    www.forbes.com/sites/dougguthrie/2013/07/31/moocs-are-toast-or-should-be/
Johnson, L., Adams Becker, S., Cummins, M., Estrada, V., Freeman, A., and Ludgate, H.
    (2013). *NMC Horizon Report: 2013 Higher Education Edition*. Austin, TX: The New
    Media Consortium.
Johnson, L., Adams Becker, S., Cummins, M., Estrada V., Freeman, A., and Ludgate, H.
    (2013). *NMC Horizon Report: 2013 K-12 Edition*. Austin, TX: The New Media
    Consortium.
Johnson, L., Adams Becker, S., Gago, D., Garcia, E., and Martín, S. (2013). *Technology
    Outlook > Latin American Higher Education 2013–2018: An NMC Horizon Project
    Regional Analysis*. Austin, TX: The New Media Consortium.
Johnson, L., Adams Becker, S., Cummins, M., Freeman, A., Ifenthaler, D., and Vardaxis,
    N. (2013). *Technology Outlook for Australian Tertiary Education 2013–2018: An NMC
    Horizon Project Regional Analysis*. Austin, TX: The New Media Consortium.
Kenrick, C. (2012). *Palo Alto Online*. "The Tsunami Online: Can e-learning revolutionize
    higher education?" From the Internet: www.paloaltoonline.com/weekly/story.php?
    story_id =17835
Kolowich, S. (2012). *Inside Higher Ed*. "MOOCs' Little Brother." From the Internet:
    www.insidehighered.com/news/2012/09/06/u-maine-campus-experiments-small-
    scale-high-touch-open-courses

Kolowich, S. (2013a). *The Chronicle of Higher Education*. "The MOOC 'Revolution' May Not Be as Disruptive as Some Had Imagined." From the Internet: https://chronicle.com/article/MOOCs-May-Not-Be-So-Disruptive/140965/

Kolowich, S. (2013b). *The Chronicle of Higher Education*. "As MOOC Debate Simmers at San Jose State, American U. Calls a Halt." From the Internet: https://chronicle.com/article/article-content/139147/

Leckart, S. (2012). *Wired*. "The Stanford Education Experiment Could Change Higher Learning Forever." From the Internet: www.wired.com/wiredscience/2012/03/ff_aiclass/all/

Lewin, T. (2013). *The New York Times*. "Master's Degree is New Frontier of Study Online." From the Internet: www.nytimes.com/2013/08/18/education/masters-degree-is-new-frontier-of-study-online.html

Liang, F. (2013). "Meet the Students—An Interview with Feynman Liang." From the Internet: www.thegoodmooc.com/2013/08/meet-students-interview-with-feynman-liang.html

Pappano, L. (2012). *The New York Times*. "The Year of the MOOC." From the Internet: www.nytimes.com/2012/11/04/education/edlife/massive-open-online-courses-are-multiplying-at-a-rapid-pace.html

Rees, J. (2013). *More or Less Bunk*. "Anti-MOOC really is the new black." From the Internet: http://moreorlessbunk.wordpress.com/2013/08/14/anti-mooc-really-is-the-new-black/

Rivard, R. (2013). *Inside Higher Ed*, "Reins on Moonlighting." From the Internet: www.insidehighered.com/news/2013/05/08/u-pennsylvania-drafts-guidelines-keep-professors-competing-against-it-online

Siemens, G. (2013). *ELearn Space*. "Neoliberalism & MOOCs: Amplifying nonsense." From the Internet: www.elearnspace.org/blog/2013/07/08/neoliberalism-and-moocs-amplifying-nonsense/

Shirky, C. (2013). *The Awl*. "Your Massively Open Offline College is Broken." From the Internet: www.theawl.com/2013/02/how-to-save-college

Shumski, D. (2013). *Education Dive*. "MOOCs by the Numbers: How Do edX, Coursera and Udacity Stack Up?" From the Internet: www.educationdive.com/news/moocs-by-the-numbers-how-do-edx-coursera-and-udacity-stack-up/161100/

Strauss, V. (2013). *The Washington Post*. "The Big Misunderstanding about MOOCs." From the Internet: www.washingtonpost.com/blogs/answer-sheet/wp/2013/02/24/the-great-divide-over-moocs/

Tapson, J. (2013). *PanoDaily.com*. "MOOCs and the Gartner Hype Cycle: A very slow tsunami." From the Internet: http://pandodaily.com/2013/09/13/moocs-and-the-gartner-hype-cycle-a-very-slow-tsunami/

Watters, A. (2012). *Hack Education*. "A Consortium of 10 Universities Announced This Week What I'm Labeling the Anti-MOOC." From the Internet: http://hackeducation.com/2012/11/16/hack-education-weekly-news-11–16–2012/

Watters, A. (2013). *Hack Education*. "Hack Education Weekly News: MOOCs and anti-MOOCs." From the Internet: www.hackeducation.com/2013/05/10/hack-education-weekly-news-5–10–2013/

Winkler, K. and Dawson, C. (2013). *Edukwest*. "MOOCs and Anti-MOOCs, Khan Academy and the Flipped Classroom." From the Internet: http://blip.tv/edukwest/review-ed-28-part-4–6-moocs-and-anti-moocs-khan-academy-and-the-flipped-classroom-6495428

5

DEVELOPING A SUSTAINABLE MOOC BUSINESS MODEL

Victor Hu

Since the launch in early 2012 of the first Silicon Valley startups offering what became known globally as Massive Open Online Courses, MOOCs have dominated media headlines and education conferences, attracted legions of both ardent supporters and fierce critics, and inspired the creation of numerous similar online learning platforms around the world. By enrolling millions of students in free courses taught by professors from internationally renowned universities, MOOCs have sparked an ongoing conversation about the future of higher education and the role of software and internet technology in its evolution. In a similarly short amount of time, MOOC platform providers have also raised hundreds of millions of dollars of capital—all without having settled on a defined business model.

The path of focusing on product development and user acquisition first, and business models and profits second, is one well worn by Silicon Valley technology companies, with famous examples such as Twitter, Instagram, and Google. It is also a strategy often encouraged by investors. With an audience of sufficient size and a product that delivers real value, the thinking goes, companies led by talented management teams can always iterate towards a sustainable business model. Nevertheless, investors must answer to their own limited partners in terms of metrics such as internal rate of return (IRR), which captures the concept of the time value of money. Once MOOC platform providers began to raise significant amounts of capital from venture capitalists, they started a clock on having to eventually create and scale a business model that can deliver to investors an acceptable return on their investment.

This chapter will present a discussion of potential MOOC business models in the context of the broader developments within the environment for education technology funding, and explore the implications for how this dynamic segment of the education industry may develop over time.

Investment in Education Technology 2.0

The emergence and funding of North American MOOC providers such as Coursera and Udacity in 2012, and similar companies in Asia, Europe, and Latin America, are only the latest manifestation of a broader trend of growing entrepreneurship and investment in education technology and services over the past three years. Historically, according to New Enterprise Associates, the venture capital industry had invested less than 3 percent of its dollars in education every year. After an initial spike during the first technology bubble, for the remainder of the 2000s, venture and growth investment in education-related companies remained relatively muted, averaging approximately $260 million per year—small relative to fields such as software technology or biotechnology, and certainly modest when contrasted against the overall size of the education industry at over $1 trillion annually in the U.S. alone. In 2012, however, early- and growth-stage investment in the sector increased to unprecedented levels of over $1 billion, according to data collected by Goldman, Sachs & Co., and in 2013 reached $1.3 billion.

What has driven this growth? Many investors believe that the education industry, which has historically been slow to change, and in which traditional models of instruction and pedagogy have persisted for centuries, is finally embracing technology and exploring new methods of teaching and learning. Catalyzed by increasing bottom-up demand—digitally native student populations that are otherwise accustomed to using technology constantly in their daily lives—institutions across both K12 and higher education are seeking to integrate technology in deeper ways into the classroom and curriculum, and in doing so are opening up new product and service opportunities to for-profit companies. At the same time, the broader education value chain is being digitized at an accelerating rate. With cloud-based learning platforms underpinned by the latest software and internet technologies, many educators are convinced that "technology-enabled education," including online courseware, is finally able to deliver acceptable learning experiences for today's students, while enabling institutions to reach students who have traditionally been educationally underserved.

These developments are accelerating innovation in the industry, as for-profit companies look to productize different components of the education value chain. Educational processes such as student recruiting or the management of admissions processes that historically were vertically integrated within the academic institution are now becoming disaggregated and unbundled. As a result, a growing number of education companies with a wide variety of business models have been created over the last half-dozen years, offering solutions such as teacher social platforms, adaptive learning algorithms, e-learning video platforms, anti-plagiarism technology and software that helps app developers access the data hidden in diverse student information systems.

Online learning, in particular, has experienced strong growth, especially at the postsecondary level. The 2013 Survey of Online Learning conducted by the Babson Survey Research Group revealed that the number of higher education students in the U.S. taking at least one online course surpassed 7.1 million in the fall of 2012, representing about one-third of all higher education students in the country. The percentage of academic leaders who rated learning outcomes in online education as the same or superior to face-to-face now stands at 74 percent. Not surprisingly then, much of the investment in education technology over the past three years has been focused on online learning.

MOOCs are only the latest phenomenon reflective of, and benefiting from, this broader investment trend. While the term 'MOOC' was coined back in 2008, and open online education has existed for decades, it was the founding and financing of two Silicon-Valley-based companies and a Boston-based nonprofit (Udacity in 2011 and Coursera and edX in 2012)—and the numerous partnerships they created with renowned universities seemingly overnight—that has catalyzed the significant media and academic attention paid to the category over the last two years, as well as the proliferation of numerous similar startups around the world.

Many Models

The business models being pursued by the current generation of education technology and online learning companies are diverse, reflecting the complexity of the learning ecosystem and the various capital pools and stakeholders that exist in the education markets. Some of these models have been borrowed from other markets and are still in the early stages of validation, while others have a long and proven history. The following overview includes examples of some of the most common approaches, and provides context for how MOOC platform provider business models may develop over time:

- *Institutional License or Subscription Model.* Companies in this category target the education budgets of institutions, and sell their software, technology or content to a K12 school or school district, a college or university, or an enterprise, typically on a per-learner or per-school basis (examples include: CompassLearning, Edmentum). Learning Management System providers, Student Information Systems and corporate e-learning content providers have utilized these models for many years, and more recently have migrated their offerings towards a Software-as-a-Service (SaaS) delivery model, charging subscription fees based on the number of students supported (examples include: Desire2Learn, Blackboard, Instructure, Ellucian, Skillsoft).
- *Individual Purchase/Subscription Model.* With the rising consumerization of education, a number of companies have created content that they sell directly to individuals or parents of students on a subscription or a la carte basis.

Content may be developed in-house, in partnership with schools or publishers, or sourced from individual instructors, and varies in type from elementary school adaptive math games to art history courses targeted at the lifelong learner (examples include: Lynda.com, Lumosity, Dreambox). In some cases, the content consists of digital textbooks that a student buys individually via a digital learning platform operated by a reseller or agent of a publisher. (Examples: CourseSmart, Kno). A derivative of this model is the App Model, whereby application publishers are monetizing individual applications that are distributed in app stores such as iTunes either through a paid download or through in-app purchases (examples: MindSnacks).

- *Freemium Model.* Following in the footsteps of popular consumer internet applications such as Dropbox and Evernote, some edtech companies distribute a lightweight version of their software application for free to individuals such as teachers or students, but offer premium, full-featured versions for a fee. In a similar approach, some companies upsell to the institution after first establishing product penetration among individuals; for example, they may provide their product to teachers and students for free while offering school districts or states a premium version to access data and analytics stemming from the use of the product in their jurisdiction (example: LearnZillion).

- *Revenue Share Model.* A number of companies who serve colleges and universities utilize a revenue sharing model through which the institutional client pays the company a fixed percentage of the tuition fees they collect from students. Typically these companies provide technology and services that enable university clients to offer degree programs online, and the fee share applies to tuition paid by students who are recruited and serviced through the company's platform and solutions (examples: 2U, Embanetcompass).

- *Sponsorship Model.* While direct advertising is rare in the education markets, a number of online learning companies have signed up corporate sponsors, thus enabling them to offer their products to students, teachers, and schools for free. In some cases the company's software platforms are white-labeled by the academic institution, but sponsors are able to derive benefit by targeting the user-base with specific marketing messages (example: Alison, Everfi).

- *Ecosystem/Platform/Marketplace Model.* Perhaps most ambitiously, a number of edtech companies are seeking to position themselves as an ecosystem or platform through which other companies such as publishers or application developers can access distribution or technology (examples: Knewton, Edmodo, Udemy). The company may operate a marketplace for supplemental online courses, or provide technology that powers such courses to make them more adaptive and personalized. In such cases, the company may charge the content or technology publisher a set percentage fee for paid applications purchased through their platform, similar to Apple's iTunes, or share in the per-seat licensing fees or course tuition earned by their partner.

As a subset of education technology players operating in the online learning category, MOOC platform providers (hereafter referred to as 'MOOC providers') face a particular challenge in monetization. One of the core aspects of the MOOC identity, and part of their perceived revolutionary nature, centers on the first "O" of its acronym: *open*. The premise is that the main product, the online course, is freely available to anyone in the world with an internet connection.

While the companies offering MOOCs have certainly contemplated the idea of charging tuition from learners directly, this defining characteristic of MOOCs has undoubtedly contributed to both their fame and popularity. Many industry participants have predicted that the impact on the industry over the long-term will be to materially reduce the cost of higher education. However, this characteristic also implies that, unless they redefine themselves—which arguably some have done already—MOOC providers must find alternatives to charging its user-base for the core product. In this context, the question that arises is whether MOOCs can find models beyond tuition or course fees that can scale truly successful businesses. The next sections examine some of the early possibilities contemplated by the MOOC providers and how some of them have responded to their experiences in the market.

Early MOOC Approaches

The initial phase of MOOC development in 2011 and 2012 focused on developing scale in partnerships and content, with no real attempt to monetize the user base. This strategy was driven in part by a belief that the marketplace for online content reflects strong network effects, where the largest audiences and highest volume of high quality courseware tend to converge. Nonetheless, the companies have clearly given thought to the business model question. In the first set of contracts signed by Coursera with university partners, for example, the company listed eight potential business models, under the heading "Possible Monetization Strategies":

- *Certification*. User pays for University-branded certificates after course completion.
- *Secure Assessments*. User pays for identify-verified testing at a private location.
- *Employee Recruiting*. Employer pays for access to students for recruiting purposes.
- *Employee or University Screening*. Employer pays to license platform for corporate training and to access employee data.
- *Human Tutoring or Grading*. User pays for tutoring, grading, or other human-provided academic support.
- *Corporate/University Enterprise Model*. Employers or schools pay for Enterprise Version of the platform.

- *Sponsorships.* Companies pay to sponsor courses and display certain advertising to users.
- *Tuition.* User pays tuition for access to the course.

These models contemplate monetizing one or more of the key assets MOOC providers possess: (i) a large and growing audience, (ii) partnerships with some of the most prestigious education brands in the world, (iii) a growing portfolio of previously inaccessible learning content, deliverable digitally at scale, and (iv) the promise of being able to collect and analyze a tremendous amount of data on students and their learning processes, including potentially identifying which students have achieved the greatest mastery of the material. Half of the models described above focus on monetizing the end user, while the other half aim to charge employers and institutions for access to technology, human capital, or audiences.

While the strategy of charging tuition is listed in the contract as an alternative, and is perhaps the most intuitive business model option, it runs contrary not only to the definition of a MOOC, as discussed previously, but also to the original visions of some of the MOOC provider founders: namely, to democratize education and make high quality education accessible to all. Indeed, much of the fanfare surrounding MOOCs in 2011 and 2012 revolved around the potential of the technology to address intractable development issues, such as emerging economies' insufficient education capacity or the problems facing the bottom of the pyramid in terms of education access. To date, the basic offerings at most of the key MOOC providers have remained free.

Premium products and services—such as verified certificates of completion, or assessments—wrapped around the core course offering are essentially market segmentation tools. They enable MOOC providers to identify the individuals who are seeking to learn not only for personal enrichment or curiosity, but who also hope to receive some form of marketplace recognition that may translate into employment, promotion, or higher salaries. To be sustainable over the long-term, this strategy rests on the assumption that MOOC providers' certificates or assessment results will carry weight in the labor markets, or convey at least incremental advantages relative to the candidate who lacks such credentials.

Some technology businesses such as Google, Autodesk, and AT&T, led by MOOC provider Udacity through a coalition known as the Open Education Alliance, are already jointly exploring how to develop standards for career readiness that will enable MOOCs to further refine their content and credentialing systems. LinkedIn, the professional social network, has recently made it easier for individuals to display such certificates on their profile pages. Through partnerships signed with a number of online learning providers—including Coursera, Udacity, and edX—learners are able to post their accomplishments to their profiles with a single click. These developments will enliven the market for alternative credentials, and over time will likely make certificates and assessment offerings from the MOOCs more valuable.

Of course, there are numerous ways to segment markets to create premium product offerings. For example, some MOOC providers differentiate between live and self-paced access; one venture-backed company, CreativeLive, records its classes in front of a live studio and an unlimited online audience, but then charges for access to recorded video content. To learn without paying, users must show up for the live broadcast much as they would for cable television programming, which is broadcast on a set schedule.

An important factor in determining the viability of these various user-focused models is the aggregate or equilibrium ratio of "serious learners" to "casual browsers"—the ones who will perhaps pay for supplemental services such as tutoring, or who approach courses with a specific employment or career advancement objective. To date, Coursera has acknowledged that the majority of its users already have degrees in higher education. Together with the widely known low completion rates most MOOCs suffer from, this suggests that the primary use case for MOOCs in its early days was curiosity-based browsing and personal enrichment. Nonetheless, it is important to note this was prior to the implementation by most MOOC providers of various premium services; as the companies grow their content base and technology platforms, their audiences will undoubtedly continue to evolve.

In an interview in 2012, Coursera's leaders noted that at the time they were actively pursuing two of the ideas listed in their first contracts: (i) charging for certificates, and (ii) serving as a recruiting matchmaker between students and companies. Later in 2012, the company stated that it was dropping its efforts to develop the recruiting business, citing scalability and demand considerations. Its certificate sales, however, have had some early traction. Launched in January of 2013 and dubbed "Signature Track," the company announced on its blog in September that it had already sold 25,000 units or $1 million. edX quickly followed suit by launching ID-verified Certificates of Achievement in October of 2013.

Other models focused on education institutions as a source of revenues are also being explored. In the early stages of MOOCs' growth in 2011 and 2012, many academics pondered what the future held for regional or local universities who did not or could not partner with a MOOC provider to offer course content or lectures. One potential answer emerged in late 2012. Coursera announced in October of that year a partnership with Antioch University, a private university with five campuses in four states focused primarily on adult learners. Under the agreement, Antioch would license certain Coursera courses and offer them to its own students for credit as part of a bachelor's degree offering. Fees paid by Antioch to Coursera would be shared with its university partners. Subsequently, the American Council on Education announced in February of 2013 that it had approved five Coursera courses for credit recommendations, further opening the door for courses on the Coursera platform to be recognized by other institutions towards granting a degree.

Then, in May of 2013, the company announced another deal with schools, this time with 10 state universities. In addition to establishing a broad partnership between the company and the schools, the agreement specified how content from those schools could be used to offer courses to students of other university partners through the Coursera platform, and detailed how revenues would be shared based on where those courses were developed and the number of students that enrolled.

The notion that the free courseware offered by content partners on a MOOC provider's platform can be used by any school as part of their core curriculum—and offered to students for credit, perhaps with school-specific bundled services—may be at once the most powerful and most disruptive use case for this category. On the one hand, it suggests that any school can utilize MOOCs to provide the online content it finds the most relevant and useful to its particular student base, while still offering instructional support, small group class discussion, a social community, and most importantly a real degree to its students. Schools theoretically can use this inter-institutional exchange of instructional content to trim costs and increase focus on areas of true differentiation and value-add, and ensure its ongoing market relevance.

On the other hand, the idea of bringing in outside (and potentially superior) content and instruction—even if it is repackaged and customized to the needs of a local college or university—is unsurprisingly quite threatening to many in the academic community, and its early implementations have already met with some controversy. Some professors have refused to participate in teaching MOOCs created by other instructors for fear of accepting a diminished role that starts a slippery slope towards perceived irrelevance. Another important question is how such an approach would impact the traditional university financial model, which historically has relied on its more profitable, large-lecture-hall introductory courses with the most "efficient" teacher-to-student ratios to subsidize more intimate and therefore costly seminar formats.

A Pivot Towards the Enterprise

Udacity, one of the well-known early pioneers in this category, provides a singular case study on the evolution of the MOOC business model. Founder and CEO Sebastian Thrun, a Stanford University research professor and Google fellow, famously predicted in 2012 that higher education in 50 years may very well be provided by no more than 10 institutions worldwide (with Udacity being a candidate for one of the 10). While the company's early vision revolved around a world in which education was free and democratized, developments over the course of the last two years have led to a shift in focus and approach.

Over its relatively short history, the company has embarked on a variety of partnerships with both universities and corporations. In January of 2013, Udacity announced a partnership with San Jose State University, whereby the company would offer low-cost courses in a number of subjects that would count toward credit at SJSU, in a bid towards addressing rising tuition, capacity constraints, and poor student performance. By September, however, the initial pilots were put on hold due to low pass rates and academic underperformance in comparison with face-to-face students (though some courses were later reinstated for further testing in December).

In May of 2013, Udacity announced a partnership with Georgia Institution of Technology and AT&T to offer a new $7,000 online master's degree in computer science. According to details released by the school, the company will receive 40 percent of revenue from the new program, and the program has ambitions to enroll as many as 10,000 students within 3 years from 300 or so current students. In announcing the program, Udacity made clear that the model it was pursuing was similar to other revenue-sharing online enablers in the space whereby the partner institution retained all admissions, academic, and degree-granting responsibilities.

As it relates to its core offering of free courses on the Udacity platform, in November of 2013, Thrun famously commented in an article published by *Fast Company* that while he had "aspired to give people a profound education," the "data was at odds with this idea" and that the students served by Udacity in pilots such as SJSU was "a group for which this medium is not a good fit." In making this observation, he also announced a shift in his approach of offering predominantly free courses to fee-based ones, as well as a move towards more vocational-based learning and corporate training versus traditional academic disciplines. As of this writing, viewing the many free courses hosted on Udacity's website without formally subscribing remains an option, while a subscription to one of the full course offerings—an option available only on a minority of the courses, and which includes in-class projects, "code reviews," personalized feedback, and verified certificates—costs between $90 and $200 per month, depending on the course.

Udacity's focus going forward appears to be on the corporate training market, which is a large, fragmented market worth $60 billion in the U.S. alone. As discussed earlier, the company has already recruited companies such as Google, Autodesk, Intuit, Nvidia, and Salesforce as "sponsors" to produce classes for the platform; these companies have also agreed to accept the certificates awarded by Udacity. Similarly, AT&T, which agreed to cover upfront costs in the rollout of the computer science program with Georgia Tech, is planning on sending many of its own employees through the program.

Coursera has also talked openly about using its platform for continuing employee development. Yahoo, for example, has paid for its employees to take MOOCs with Coursera using its Signature Track program. The company has also discussed the possibility of selling dashboards or analytic tools to companies to help them track employees' progress with online courses.

Open Source, LMS, and Other Possibilities

Despite being a nonprofit, edX has also pursued a number of revenue opportunities that shed light on other potentially sustainable models for MOOCs. Besides following in the direct-to-consumer path of offering certificates of achievement, the organization has developed several enterprise-facing approaches. It already hosts and administers courses for organizations such as the International Finance Corporation for a fee. In September of 2013, edX announced Open edX, an open-source platform for MOOCs, to be built in partnership with Google. The goal of the project is to enable corporations, universities, and individuals alike to create online courses. The nonprofit has announced partnerships with countries such as France and China, and will provide ongoing technical support and services for a fee. The open-source approach, which is used by software vendors such as Red Hat, is predominantly a services model, whereby companies sell subscriptions for ongoing support, training, and integration services that help customers in using the open-source software. edX's approach to date is to encourage more institutions to become content producers by giving every institution access to an open-source platform to experiment with different ways to produce and share content.

The massive audience that MOOCs have attracted to date suggest a variety of other possible ways to monetize. MOOC providers could provide linkages for students who completed and enjoyed their first online course to schools that offer online degrees, in a lead-generation model. Similarly, alongside produced courses, MOOC providers could sell complementary content products such as digital textbooks from publishers. Blackboard, for example, the largest LMS player in U.S. higher education, recently announced an initiative to create an online store for textbooks that would allow students to purchase and access digital content in one place.

A different institution-centric approach lies in the world of learning management systems (LMS). When Coursera raised its Series B round of $43 million in July of 2013, the company discussed its intention to add a series of additional features to broaden the learning platform, including mobile applications, social collaboration tools, and third-party app integrations. As MOOC providers enhance the software infrastructure features of their platforms, they will increasingly overlap with the traditional LMS, which has historically been licensed to the institution or sold through a SaaS model. This market, while relatively mature in the U.S. higher education sector, has a proven market size and use case; over time the LMS has become the basic software infrastructure that virtually all schools utilize to deliver and track courses online.

Generally, the LMS has not included content; that was traditionally supplied by the instructor or publisher. However, in the wake of the media frenzy surrounding MOOCs over the last few years, a number of the largest LMS providers have created new platforms to host open courseware. The advantage that MOOC platform providers bring with them in this landscape lies in its established partnerships and a library of content created by those partners. With the development of additional infrastructure and software features, MOOC platforms may well be on a head-on collision course with the LMS.

Conclusion

As MOOCs continue to evolve, a foreseeable challenge lies in the potentially divergent objectives of the companies providing the technology and services platforms with the university content providers. University partners, who are generally nonprofit, are experimenting with online education for a variety of reasons: to stay abreast of current technology trends and ensure longer term relevance; to promote their brands and extend the reach of their institutions and professors; and to improve their research and pedagogy on campus. At the same time, these schools have a vested interest in protecting their brands and intellectual property. MOOC platform providers, on the other hand, as venture capitalists' portfolio companies, are structured and incentivized to create a financial return for their investors, including by disrupting existing markets. Already, some university partners, nervous about the longer term implications of giving away their content through MOOCs, or under pressure from their faculty, have begun to pull back. How these structural dynamics play out over time remains to be seen.

What remains clear, however, is that change will continue to happen in this category at an accelerated pace. Just in the last two years, euphoria and apprehension about MOOCs' growth and potential impact have already given way in large part to a mixture of disappointment and relief over their perceived failures. At the same time, MOOC providers have experimented with over half a dozen different business models, as described above, with mixed results. What they have done successfully is attract a massive audience and collect a tremendous amount of data, which over time will deepen the industry's collective understanding of what factors contribute to better teaching and learning. Whether MOOCs will eventually become the core building block on which the majority of higher education courses are built is still an open question, but the outsized role they will likely play in promoting stronger learning outcomes is already starting to be seen.

Suggested Reading

Chafkin, M. "Udacity's Sebastian Thrun, Godfather of Free Online Education, Changes Course," *Fast Company*, December 2013. Available at www.fastcompany.com/3021473/udacity-sebastian-thrun-uphill-climb

Goldman, Sachs & Co., per data gathered by the Investment Banking Division.

"Grade Change: Tracking Online Education in the United States," Babson Survey Research Group, January 2014.

Kolowich, S. "San Jose State U. Puts MOOC Project with Udacity on Hold," *The Chronicle of Higher Education*, July 19, 2013. Available at http://chronicle.com/article/San-Jose-State-U-Puts-MOOC/140459/

Protalinski, E. "Coursera Partners with 10 New US Universities Not Just for Online Courses, but to Add Mooc to Their Classes Too," *The Next Web*, May 30, 2013. Available at http://thenextweb.com/insider/2013/05/30/coursera-partners-with-10-new-us-universities-not-just-for-online-courses-but-to-add-mooc-to-their-classes-too/

Rivard, R. "Blackboard Goes MOOC," *Inside Higher Ed*, July 11, 2013. Available at www.insidehighered.com/news/2013/07/11/blackboard-largest-provider-classroom-management-software-enters-mooc-fray#sthash.5lLd5pdr.dpbs

Sakoda, J. "A Crisis in Education is a Terrible Thing to Waste," *New Enterprise Associates*, November 3, 2012. Available at http://50.57.73.192/blog/a-crisis-in-education-is-a-terrible-thing-to-waste

Simonite, T. "As Data Floods In, Massive Open Online Courses Evolve," *MIT Technology Review*, June 5, 2013. Available at www.technologyreview.com/news/515396/as-data-floods-in-massive-open-online-courses-evolve/

"The attack of the MOOCs," *The Economist*, July 20, 2013. Available at www.economist.com/news/business/21582001-army-new-online-courses-scaring-wits-out-traditional-universities-can-they

Young, J. "Inside the Coursera Contract: How an Upstart Company Might Profit From Free Courses," *The Chronicle of Higher Education*, July 19, 2012. Available at http://chronicle.com/article/How-an-Upstart-Company-Might/133065/

6

THE SUBJECT MATTERS

MOOCs and Relevancy

Dennis Yang and Meg Evans

In rural Mexico, students are improving their conversational English with the help of a seasoned teacher based in the Canary Islands.[1] In Lagos, Nigeria, Maureen Iyasele is better managing her youth development center thanks to a course from Steve Blank, a seasoned entrepreneur in Silicon Valley. In Kathmandu, Nepal, Uma Adhikari is making strides at work, because of his learning from an expert Oracle teacher in Lisbon. MOOCs have made this possible.

The best teachers have the power to change lives. Reflecting on most impactful educators in one's own life, the list likely includes classroom teachers, coaches, mentors, bosses, and friends. Sal Khan, for example, as a hedge-fund analyst, would likely not have been invited to create a MOOC. Yet, about 10 million a students a month learn everything from number sense to the French Revolution from the unassuming finance professional. But what about the potential Sal Khans of the world who don't have web skills and access to influential networks? What about that great mentor who taught you the ropes in your profession?

To unleash the power of MOOCs we need to expand the understanding of the "open" in Massively Open Online Courses, as not only open to all learners, but open to all teachers from all cultures and localized contexts.

MOOCs have provided a peek behind the walls of the once-guarded elite institutions of higher education, but many have rightly pointed out the colonial nature of this assumption that everyone *should* be taught by Harvard and other "elite" faculty. Gianpierto Pertriglieri, a Harvard Business School professor points out: "MOOCs aren't digital keys to great classrooms' doors. At best, they are infomercials for those classrooms. At worst they are digital postcards from gated communities" (Petriglieri, 2013).

The Potential for Impact

Stories like that of "The Boy Wonder of Ulan Bator" (Battushig Myanganbayar, a Mongolian teen who, after acing MIT's Circuits and Electronics, enrolled at the same engineering mecca this past fall) are anomalies (Pappano, 2013). Youth unemployment in Mongolia is hovering at 16 percent (ILO 2013). While MOOCs have helped Myanganbayar get to MIT, they will not help 1 out of 5 of his classmates who are unable to find a job.

Mongolia's youth unemployment rate is in the second quartile globally. More than a third of countries for which we have employment data have youth unemployment rates of over 20 percent. At the top, that percentage grows as high as 73 percent.

According to the International Labour Organization, employment grew to 202 million people globally, up 5 million from the previous year (Global, 2014). Concurrently many companies are unable to find qualified applicants. In China, 74 percent of employers have said they have positions they can't fill. In Brazil, that number is 63 percent and in Russia it's 57 percent (Herzog, 2014). Youth unemployment in all of these countries is above 15 percent. The problem is not entirely one of job creation; it's also one of job preparedness.

Even once employed, graduates and employers alike have learned the hard way that a degree does not mean job preparedness. Only 42 percent of employers believe that new graduates are ready for work, whereas 72 percent of educational institutions felt their students were entering the workforce prepared (Mourshed et al., 2012).

Technological advances have led to structural changes to the economy; workers must continue training to stay relevant (Bryniolfsson & McAfee, 2012). As a hiring specialist puts it in a Thomas Friedman article, "In the new economy, 'you have to prove yourself. A degree document is no longer a proxy for the competency employers need.' Too many of the 'skills you need in the workplace today are not being taught by colleges'" (Friedman, 2013).

Battushig's experience shows the promise of the medium to gain access to greater opportunity, but how do we make his experience more commonplace?

Local Solutions

If MOOCs are to have a real impact on significant global issues of unemployment and workforce development, the future must be one in which we teach what matters at a local-level. In Mongolia, the mining and agriculture industries dominate the market. How can the medium that helped Battushig also help his classmate looking for a job at the top Mongolian mining company? In China, skilled workers must understand electronic components and semiconductors. With such diversity in demographics and driving industries, content must be responsive to individual countries' challenges.

To be clear, this need to train workers for specific localized industry is not an unrecognized need, training centers and workforce development programs exist around the world. However, the traditional train-the-trainer models are reliant upon costly in-person seminars, limited by the availability of capable instructors, cost, and student's ability to travel. In the developed world, these trainers may not have expertise in the right area, given rapidly shifting content needs. The potential impact of MOOCs here is significant. There is an opportunity for employers to make a difference here—either creating their own online courses to screen applicants for the skills necessary for the job or to simply make clear the skills and training necessary.

As MOOCs evolve, it is worth asking of online courses—will this help someone change their daily wages, stay in their existing job, or find a new job? Will it help them find jobs in the industries that matter to their communities? What are the endemic skillsets and critical experiences from the older working generations that should be shared with the younger members of the workforce?

These skillsets needn't be limited to technical skills. At the Universidad Michoacana de San Nicolás de Hidalgo in Mexico, the administration, intent on both rural development and indigenous studies, produced their own MOOC to capture local art traditions. The feather mosaic and maize-based sculptures were near extinction, but now, through a Udemy MOOC, students not only in Michoacán but throughout the Spanish-speaking world will have access to the instruction of these great masters.

Ultimately, it is not those of us here in the U.S. who should dictate what students *should* be learning in Mongolia, Mexico, or Nigeria. This decision ought to lie with student demand. The course topics of MOOCs have thus far been largely dependent on which professors are interested in teaching and their subject-level expertise. How do we move to a system in which course topics are created in response to student interest?

We at Udemy believe this will happen in a marketplace model, which relies on social proof. With students able to solicit instructors from whom they want to learn and rate the quality of the courses they've taken, the marketplace matures to meet student demand.

Student Motivation

This question of demand-driven content is predicated on a broader idea that students will be motivated to take courses that have real impact on their earning potential, job development, or personal enrichment. It is worth exploring this question of motivation more in-depth.

Much has been written about the failure of MOOCs based on low course completion rates. This may be an unfair stone to cast for it does not take into account the question—how many people entered the course hoping to finish? What was the motivation to enroll? Did they in fact reach their learning objectives?

When we asked students who were more than half way through a course the question, "Has Udemy helped you achieve your learning goals?" 92 percent of respondents answered in the affirmative. As our understanding of MOOCs evolves, so do the metrics by which we look at success and quality.

Course engagement largely tracks to the intention of enrolling. When we surveyed our students, we found that 90 percent came to learn practical knowledge—30 percent of users surveyed came to build something (i.e. a website, app), 25 percent came with the intention of developing skills to shift careers or prepare for an examination, 25 percent came to hone their skills, and 10 percent came for help with a start-up or business.

Take, for example, Carlos Andres Obando. Carlos lives in Ibarra, Ecuador where he studied engineering, planning to work on the process of aiding the automation of industry. Carlos was also interested in app development, but struggled to find quality content in Spanish. He found Udemy and took three Spanish iOS courses. Carlos is now the founder of Talov App Studio, his own design company, working full time on app development in Ibarra.

Maureen Iyasele provides another great illustration; she works tirelessly in Lagos, Nigeria to help connect young job-seekers to great positions. She started her non-profit, drop-in youth development organization in 2011, and in only a few years she has served 5,000 unemployed students who walk in off the street. She credits the ability to run her organization effectively to a host of MOOCs she's taken on entrepreneurship, operations management, and personal branding.

Given that Udemy is a mixture of paid and free courses, the motivational data above makes clear what students were willing to pay for. Udemy students are both intrinsically and extrinsically motivated. Some took courses to get that raise coming up, while others took courses because they had an interest in creating a website for their church or local non-profit.

Instructor Motivation

We must ask the same motivational questions of teachers. Why do teachers teach? Again the answer is both intrinsic and extrinsic. When we surveyed our instructors we found that most were motivated by the desire to teach and share their knowledge. But creating a course takes time and effort and we've seen that extrinsic motivation—the prospect of being able to charge a nominal amount for their course—has also driven course creation. Rather than move through a university structure, teachers are directly rewarded for quality teaching. In this new model, teaching can become a sustainable income source for local experts if teachers want to charge. Teachers set prices by looking at comparable offerings in the market place.

The course Carlos took, "Programación iOS para iPhone y iPad," was taught by Fernando Rodriguez, a lifelong technology educator. He had the expertise to teach the course, but the motivation came when he saw that instructors teaching similar courses in English had found success. Given the potential profit *and* impact, he took the time to create a great course that helped change Carlos' life.

Ultimately, the learning ecosystem must be sustainable. It can't be perpetually externally funded—we must leverage the interests of the students to drive not only content creation, but also funding for teachers to teach.

Udemy Global

We are trying to tackle a piece of this global education puzzle at Udemy, guided by the mission of democratizing teaching and learning. We create an even playing field for educators with a platform that makes it easy for anyone to create an online course and publish into a broader marketplace. An indigenous artist from Morelia Mexico, a science teacher from Long Beach, and a 70-year-old British copywriter all use Udemy to teach and scale their message.

For our millions of students we aim to make top-quality learning content from the world's experts dramatically more affordable for anyone, anywhere. As of May 2014, we have 14,000 courses in the marketplace, ranging from Portuguese courses for Brazilian entrepreneurs from Endeavor Brazil to HIV/AIDs prevention courses in Setswana from TeachAIDS. Each month we add about 1,000 new courses to the marketplace.

Interest is clear. Currently, 60 percent of our site visitors are from outside the United States and that percentage has grown steadily over the past 6 months. These visitors are from over 190 countries and territories. Udemy has been translated into 11 languages and we are working with partners to bring relevant content to communities around the world. Native mobile applications for iOS and Android enable offline downloading so that reliable internet connection does not become a pre-requisite to effective learning.

For example, in rural Mexico, in the Michoacán state, tablets pre-loaded with MOOCs are rotated between 3 schools so that the maximum number of students can learn from the resources. The courses, all taught in Spanish, range from English language instruction to personal empowerment. The courses come from passionate teachers and individuals everywhere from Texas to the Canary Islands.

Conclusion

We are just beginning to tap the potential of online learning and MOOCs in the developing world, but it's important to note that MOOCs are not a panacea. They must be part of a broader strategy to increase access to affordable and applicable education that includes primary school development, blended learning, apprenticeships, and mentoring.

We continue to think about the best ways to deliver online learning to students around the world. Whether it is video or something else, we hope to be in the forefront of innovating what is next. We challenge ourselves to continue to find better ways to enable the best teachers around the world to reach hundreds of millions of students around the world.

Note

1   Students are in the Michoacán state, attending a school in Paracho.

References

Brynjolfsson, E., & McAfee, A. (2012). *Race against the machine: how the digital revolution is accelerating innovation, driving productivity, and irreversibly transforming employment and the economy*. Lexington, MA: Digital Frontier Press.

Country Comparison: Unemployment, Youth Ages 15–24 (n.d.). Central Intelligence Agency. Retrieved May 6, 2014, from www.cia.gov/library/publications/the-world-factbook/rankorder/2229rank.html?countryname=Mongolia&countrycode=mg(r)ion Code=eas&rank=57#mg

Friedman, T. (2013, May 28). How to Get a Job. *The New York Times*. Retrieved May 6, 2014, from www.nytimes.com/2013/05/29/opinion/friedman-how-to-get-a-job.html?_r=0

Global Employment Trends 2014: risk of a jobless recovery? (2014). Geneva: International Labour Organization.

International Labour Organization (2013). Youth Employment Challenges in Mongolia. Retrieved January 2014 from www.ilo.org/wcmsp5/groups/public/---asia/---ro-bangkok/---ilo-beijing/documents/publication/wcms_220929.pdf

Herzog, C. S. (2014, January 6). Skills Gaps Holding Back the Global Economy [Infographic]. Retrieved May 6, 2014, from www.diplomaticourier.com/blog/1984-skills-gaps-holding-back-the-global-economy

Mourshed, M., Farrell, D., & Barton, D. (2012). Education to Employment: Designing a System that Works. McKinsey Center for Government. Retrieved May 6, 2014, from http://mckinseyonsociety.com/downloads/reports/Education/Education-to-Employment_FINAL.pdf

Pappano, L. (2013, September 14). The Boy Genius of Ulan Bator. *The New York Times*. Retrieved May 6, 2014, from www.nytimes.com/2013/09/15/magazine/the-boy-genius-of-ulan-bator.html?_r=0

Petriglieri, G. (2013, October 9). Let Them Eat MOOCs. *Harvard Business Review*. Retrieved May 6, 2014, from http://blogs.hbr.org/2013/10/let-them-eat-moocs/

7

NOVOED, A SOCIAL LEARNING ENVIRONMENT

Farnaz Ronaghi, Amin Saberi, and Anne Trumbore

Learning is a social act. And yet for most students, their experience with a Massive Open Online Course (MOOC) is watching a video, taking multiple-choice tests or quizzes, and possibly reading forum posts, which can be anonymous. This experience is more interactive than reading a textbook, but far less interactive than working with one's peers to create a shared understanding of knowledge. It does not allow for any kind of true collaboration or meaningful social connection around course content. What the technological design of most MOOCs has allowed us to do is to take the most boring and ineffective part of learning and put it online for students to complete in the most inhospitable environment for education—isolation.

NovoEd began as a solution to this problem. Stanford's Professor Chuck Eesley wanted to offer the popular Stanford course, *Technology Entrepreneurship*, as a MOOC, but none of the existing technologies allowed him to scale up his on-campus active learning teaching techniques in which students work together and learn by doing—in this case, creating a start-up. He asked fellow professor Amin Saberi, whose research focuses on the intersection of computer and social sciences, if Amin could design a new learning environment for his online course. With the help of Amin's Ph.D. student, Farnaz Ronaghi, they built a prototype and over 150,000 students have taken *Technology Entrepreneurship* to date.

The NovoEd online learning environment uses techniques in human–computer interaction, algorithms, and social network design to foster online peer learning and help students perfect their problem solving, leadership, and communication skills. The many MOOCs hosted on NovoEd since late 2012 have provided valuable data used to refine technology and class design to provide a connected, effective, and engaging learning experience for students. This experience is not limited to granting students access to incredible educational content, but is instead enhanced by real access to other students around the world. By harnessing the power of the social web, we are amplifying the potential of students to create meaningful change in their lives.

The quality as well as the quantity of student work produced in these courses is inspiring. Within 12 months, students in free and open courses hosted on NovoEd produced over 150,000 presentations, videos, projects, business models, and essays, and half a million instances of peer grading. Each of these assignments represents higher order thinking such as creation and synthesis, and the act of their production clearly demonstrates that when students are empowered by technology and design to create work that requires them to synthesize course material, and not just master it, they rise to the challenge even in the absence of traditional modes of certification and motivation.

These MOOCs, which maximized social connection, enabled collaboration, and active, project-based learning, show us that online educational environments have tremendous potential to enhance student learning if we design them to maximize student involvement and peer-to-peer learning. A crucial component of student engagement is feeling connected to, and supported by, a learning community. Therefore, we have designed NovoEd's technology, and the pedagogy of the courses hosted on it, to maximize these connections and support. Results are promising. When we compare the number of students who complete the first assignment in these MOOCs to those who satisfy instructors' grading criteria for completion, we find that 33 percent–63 percent of students persist in completing these courses.

Design of Technology

NovoEd's online learning environment was created to amplify student engagement. Designed from inception to put student interaction and collaboration at the center of the learning experience, NovoEd's technology encourages active and peer learning through team based exercises, calibrated peer evaluation and feedback, visible student work, forums for exchange of ideas, as well as direct communication between students. Every course home page displays student activity to create a dynamic environment that is responsive to students and their work. When students go to class, they see students and teams who are currently active on the site, student work which is being looked at or commented on by other students, and trending forum threads. This visible activity shifts the focus from instructor-created content to student-created content and presents the course as an ongoing learning event. Almost every student action on the platform is transparent and is reflected on a student's profile page to create accountability and a sense of belonging to the course community. Profiles include a student's reputation or engagement score, team (if applicable), submissions, forum activity, endorsements, network, courses taken, number of peer reviews, and number of peer reviews that were rated by their recipients as helpful. The profile helps others assess the engagement level, as well as style and quality of work of the learner, especially at the time of team formation. Teams also have their own profile page and collaborative workspace where students can post and comment on assignments.

This technology allows us to teach online in ways we have never been able to before. Once we shift the focus from content delivery to student learning, we enable a range of teaching practices that scaffold peer-to-peer instruction, project-based learning, formation of networked learning communities, and learner autonomy. In the on-campus classroom, part of an instructor's role can be to make thinking visible. In the project-based MOOCs in the NovoEd online learning environment, the technology and design assume this role, leaving the instructor more latitude to facilitate thinking and to participate in the learning community as both guide and fellow learner. When the "sage leaves the stage," instructors are freed from controlling content flow to students and can instead focus on creating the conditions for interactions among students that promote engagement, content synthesis, and creation of course work.

Reputation and Accountability to Community

In order to create a culture of accountability and transparency, NovoEd uses a reputation system called TeamRank to help students see how their activity in the course influences their standing in the learning community. While the exact formula used to determine it varies from course to course, TeamRank is an aggregation of the contributions of the learner to each team assignment, to the forums, and to the peer evaluation process, as well as grades on assignments. When students participate in a team assignment, they are typically asked to evaluate their teammates' contributions at the time of submission. Therefore, a student's reputation will be a function of the quality of their coursework (often peer-reviewed) and their teammates' valuation weighted by their reputation. In this sense, TeamRank is very similar to the PageRank™ mechanism employed by Google and other search engines for computing the popularity of a webpage.

Team Formation and Opportunities for Peer Learning

Formation of teams has a clear and positive effect on both engagement and completion. Students surveyed ranked the opportunity to work in teams and form networks with other students as one of the most valuable aspects of the course experience. Instructors have used online teams either as small workshop groups where each student submitted their assignment individually, or as working groups where one project is created and submitted collectively. Both approaches enabled students to form a personalized network of fellow learners within the larger class cohort: the network remains manageable in size regardless of the number of total students enrolled in the class.

NovoEd supports two types of team formation processes: algorithmic and organic. Algorithmic teams are formed automatically based on criteria set by the instructor, and are often transient as they are formed around a particular assignment and are dissolved afterwards. Organic teams are formed by learners themselves and may persist through the course, although students can leave one team and join another at any time. (The option to form a "team of one" is also available). Students find each other through searching submitted assignments, answers to course profile questions, location, and key words on the profile. This activity reinforces the notion of the class as a community of learners who are working towards similar if not unified learning goals. At a technological level, a clustering algorithm is employed that partitions learners based on their profile information, demographics, and activity level. The clustering method can provide cohesion or diversity across certain attributes and is applied directly to form algorithmic teams. In organic team formation, it is used as a recommendation system to suggest potential teammates to learners.

The most explicit and formalized opportunity for peer learning is peer grading. When instructors add peer grading to project-based assignments, with a rubric that supports students in critical evaluation, they not only create a connection between students and the work of their peers, but also expand a student's identity as learner to include an identity as an evaluator. Students who are given the chance to evaluate each other's work are given the opportunity to think like experts about a topic. This task not only enables deeper understanding of the material, but also completes a cognitive loop to promote the development of critical thinking skills. In addition, peer grading encourages and facilitates higher levels of student interaction and engagement by requiring the student to look closely at other student work, to act as both creator and evaluator of course work, and to support the development of autonomous and empowered learning.

Creation of Course Community through Project-Based Learning

The multiple opportunities for collaboration and peer learning through both technological capabilities and course design can foster a clear sense of learning community for many students. Many instructors leverage these elements to create engaging project-based learning experiences at scale. Assignments are designed to be faithful to the content being taught with real world applications: connected, explicitly building knowledge used to complete future assignments; and student-driven, as students had ultimate latitude to choose how, when, and whether to participate in the assignment. The cohesion of these elements creates numerous opportunities for students to engage broadly and deeply with course content and each other to synthesize their knowledge and develop both personal and shared understanding of the content and its applications in a variety of contexts. Through this cohesion, students move beyond mastery of content to develop higher-order skills through the production of complex, meaningful, and authentic projects such as videos, presentations, flyers, detailed, multi-media analyses, and more. Clear and consistent communication from the instructor and teaching team throughout the course assists in defining the learning experience for students as a community event. Weekly emails with encouragement about, and instructions for, working with course content directly correlate to more student engagement, even though these emails may be composed well in advance. Some instructors have commented directly on displayed student work to strengthen the foundations of the learning community.

Crash Course on Creativity MOOC

Tina Seelig's Crash Course on Creativity exemplifies the possibilities of student-centered, project-based learning at scale. Offered through Stanford University, the course was designed for anyone interested in exploring and expanding their own creative process. The learning goals for students included exploring factors that stimulate and inhibit creativity in individuals, teams, and organizations and creating an understanding of how these factors influence themselves and their peers in the course.

In order to facilitate these goals, the course design was project-based, team-based, and experiential. Lectures were minimized and student-generated work was emphasized as both a learning outcome and a focal text of the course.

The course was notable for the subject matter (which begs the question, "how do you teach creativity?"), the diversity of projects, and the vibrancy and sensitivity of the learning community. Each week, students watched a 2–6 minute lecture that provided context and established the learning goals for the assignment, as well as reinforcing the idea that the students would learn by doing the assignment. In order to do the assigned projects, students had to experience the breakdown of their own creative inhibitions, making explicit for themselves the implicit assumptions that inhibit creativity. This series of group and individual assignments helped create conditions for a connected community where creative risk-taking was supported and encouraged. Non-anonymous peer review not only allowed students to practice "thinking like an expert" about creativity and become evaluators as well as creators, but also served as a formalized opportunity to form connections within the class. Many students developed and explored their identities as creative risk-takers and learners on their profile pages, through their assignments and in their teams and team workspaces. The visibility of identity and social presence created a learning community which was safe enough for 2,300 students to submit an optional final assignment: a "failure resume" viewable by all enrolled students.

Ultimately, students created over 25,000 projects to fulfill course assignments, including mind maps, generating 100 solutions to a problem, and a book cover of their autobiography, among others. Of the 28,000 students who enrolled, approximately 6,500 completed the first assignment. And of these, 45.6 percent (about 3,000) satisfied the grading criteria to receive a statement of accomplishment.

Technology Entrepreneurship MOOCs

Chuck Eesley's *Technology Entrepreneurship Parts 1 and 2* successfully blended academic content with real-world practice while creating the conditions under which students could find and connect with peers worldwide to create projects with direct applications inside the online classroom and outside in the physical world. Offered through Stanford University, the course was designed for anyone with an interest in developing an understanding of technology entrepreneurship and has a globally diverse enrollment of engaged participants.

The learning goals for students were ambitious. By the end of the course, students were able to articulate a process for taking a technology idea and finding a high-potential commercial opportunity, create and verify a plan for gathering resources such as talent and capital, and create and verify a business model for how to sell and market an entrepreneurial idea. In order to achieve these goals, students worked in teams to gain practical experience to better understand the theory of the fundamentals of technology entrepreneurship.

The design of the course, with its mix of expertly curated content from a variety of academic and non-academic sources, successful industry mentors, focus on student-generated work, and "guide to the side" presence of the instructor, created ideal conditions for active learning. Each assignment clearly built into the final project, and the instructor made these connections explicit in his communication. Students who enrolled in Part 2 of the course re-formed their teams in the first week, and refined and expanded their project from Part 1 throughout the whole of the course. Perhaps because the final projects of each course have perceived and sometimes recognized monetary value outside the classroom (some ventures developed in iterations of this course have been funded by venture capital), the mix of academic study and industry practice in course design encourages and empowers students to create value for themselves rather than accept the instructor's definition of value.

Of the approximately 20,000 students who enrolled in Part 1, around 1,700 completed the first assignment. And of these, 50.8 percent (about 900) satisfied the grading criteria to receive a statement of accomplishment. Part 2 saw 6,000 students enroll, 900 submit the first assignment, and almost 600 receive a statement of accomplishment for a 62.4 percent completion rate.

Higher-Order Engagement

We have seen this pattern of student engagement and collaboration in many MOOCs across disciplines. When instructors leverage social and collaborative technologies to allow for experiential learning worldwide, students respond even in the absence of traditional incentives such as credit, certificates, or degrees.

What students report as extremely important in MOOCs with high engagement are the projects they create with the help of their peers. When social technologies are combined with instructional practices such as project-based learning and non-anonymous peer review, the resulting online learning environment amplifies some of the most beneficial aspects of peer-to-peer learning. For instance, students often rank the ability to see each other's work and comment on it as one of the most valuable aspects of MOOCs hosted on NovoEd. What happens when we apply this finding to the instructional design of the on-campus classroom? Much is made of the value of the social connections formed at elite institutions of higher learning, but how often do students at these institutions get to truly learn from their peers by evaluating or considering their intellectual work? One clear benefit of the MOOC explosion is the knowledge of how students use technology and course content to create their own pathways to learning. What we have observed is that when students have access not only to course content, but also each other, then they create surprising connections and often extraordinary work.

Real-World Results

Successful startups that have come out of the Chuck Eesley's Technology Entrepreneurship MOOC include *TommyJams* in India, *Stylemarks* in Germany, *Terafold Biologics* in the US/Chile, and *Ranktab* in Mexico. Teachers from school districts in Seattle, Los Angeles, and others are collaborating on implementation practices for Common Core Standards in Kenji Hakuta's Constructive Classroom Conversations: Mastering Language for the Common Core State Standards. Students report that they have changed careers after creating portfolios of creative work in a Crash Course in Creativity, Design Thinking Action Lab, and Storytelling for Change. Small companies and large corporations alike are having their employees enroll in NovoEd MOOCs and work on virtual and real-world teams, sometimes simultaneously. When we harness the power of the social web to outstanding educational content and innovative technological and pedagogical design for free, we are closer to achieving the dream of quality education for all.

Beyond MOOCS

MOOCs begin to make good on their massive promises when we think creatively about how to use the lessons we have learned from them. Now that we can create online learning environments in which students may realize their own potential for success through their own work, how can we encourage the formation of learning communities and networks, and engaged communities of practice? How can we integrate technology into physical classrooms so that they become truly blended and more than the sum of on-campus classroom plus online component? How can we support the lifelong learning which is becoming increasingly necessary for success in the twenty-first-century workplace? How can we democratize success instead of just access?

I. Lifelong Learning

Today's continuously evolving workspace requires employees to change and grow at a rapid pace. Both mid-level managers and front-line employees must be given meaningful opportunities to grow and develop the necessary skills of virtual teamwork, collaboration, communication, and creativity if companies wish to retain and attract talented, skilled employees and increase their market share. But providing instruction and support to develop these critical employees has been impossible at scale until recently. A growing number of companies are offering their employees SPOCs as well as organized participation in MOOCs to provide engaging, high quality content that they can learn and work with in the company of their coworkers. When employees are given the opportunity to work together on projects with direct application to their specific work situations, they rapidly develop the skills necessary to twenty-first-century leadership: creativity, collaboration, critical thinking, and communication.

II. Back to the Future

Small Private Online Courses (SPOCs) allow motivated, committed, and geographically diverse students to learn together at lower costs and higher convenience. A number of innovative institutions are already experimenting with SPOCs in executive education, continuing studies, and business education. For example, the 8-week Startup CEO hosted on NovoEd in the winter of 2014 saw 330 enrolled students hailing from every continent (except Antarctica). 40 percent had C-suite positions, 30 percent were working CEOs, 46 percent were working on their own startup with 1–9 employees, 66 percent had college degrees, and 45 percent had graduate degrees. Through their diverse talents and experiences, these students created an invaluable network of learners and a true community of practice as they shared best practices and advice in formal and informal ways.

III. Blended Learning Environments

While flipping the classroom enables students to take lectures home, blending the classroom with social and collaborative technologies expands the walls of the physical classroom by blurring the boundaries between the classroom learning environment, the online learning environment, and the students' social lives, which are themselves already blended with social and collaborative technologies.

Institutions such as the Carnegie Foundation for the Advancement of Teaching are pioneering the use of social online learning environments to connect on-campus students online so that they can engage in knowledge-making and productive struggle in a technology mediated environment. This expansion makes student thinking and interaction around course content visible in ways that are impossible to measure accurately and consistently track in the physical classroom. The data recorded in these environments, both qualitative and quantitative, will improve teaching and learning practices not just on a class by class basis, but also nationwide.

Going Forward

As innovative instances of using online learning environment proliferate, they encourage new ways of thinking about what it means to learn, to teach, and to become a learner outside the physical classroom. Each new experiment raises many questions, including:

- How can we use the emerging cultural practices of online learning communities to design more effective online teaching practices?
- How can we surface data from online learning to instructors so that they may use it in class?
- What are efficient and effective ways of measuring learning outcomes? Lower order learning like retrieval is easier to define and measure while we have yet to quantify higher order learning like critical thinking and creativity.
- How do we provide real-time support to learners based on predictive models of behavior?

For the first time in history, we have the capability to amplify social learning by connecting students across geographical boundaries and engaging them with sensible use of technology and design. There is a revolution in learning coming, but it will not arrive as we have predicted. Revolutions, like true learning, don't happen in isolation and they don't happen from the top down. When we see a revolution in online learning, it will come from our students, when they have the technology to create connection and meaning to change their own lives.

Suggested Reading

Barron, B., & Darling-Hammond, L. (2008). Teaching for meaningful learning: A review of research on inquiry-based and cooperative learning. *Powerful Learning: What We Know about Teaching for Understanding*, 11–70.

Couros, A. (2010). Developing personal learning networks for open and social learning. *Emerging Technologies in Distance Education*, 109–128.

Garrison, D. R., & Cleveland-Innes, M. (2005). Facilitating cognitive presence in online learning: Interaction is not enough. *The American Journal of Distance Education*, 19(3), 133–148.

Eesley, C. (2014, February 11). Behold: A virtual course without online ed's huge dropout rate. *Bloomberg Business Week.* Retrieved June 5, 2014, from www.businessweek.com/articles/2014-02-11/behold-a-virtual-course-without-online-eds-huge-dropout-rate

Grover, S., Franz, P., Schneider, E., & Pea, R. (2013, June). The MOOC as distributed intelligence: Dimensions of a framework for the design and evaluation of MOOCs. In *Proceedings of the 10th International Conference on Computer Supported Collaborative Learning,* Madison, WI, 16–19. Retrieved November 2013, from http://lytics.stanford.edu/wordpress/wp-content/uploads/2013/04/Framework-for-Design-Evaluation-of-MOOCs-Grover-Franz-Schneider-Pea_final.pdf

Kulkarni, C., Wei, K. P., Le, H., Chia, D., Papadopoulos, K., Cheng, J., . . . & Klemmer, S. R. (2013). Peer and self assessment in massive online classes. *ACM Transactions on Computer-Human Interaction (TOCHI), 20*(6), 33.

Sadler, P. M., & Good, E. (2006). The impact of self-and peer-grading on student learning. *Educational Assessment, 11*(1), 1–31.

Smith, K. A., Sheppard, S. D., Johnson, D. W., & Johnson, R. T. (2005). Pedagogies of engagement: Classroom-based practices. *Journal of Engineering Education, 94*(1), 87–101.

Spiro, R. J. (1988). Cognitive Flexibility Theory: Advanced knowledge acquisition in ill-structured domains. *Technical Report No. 441.*

Treisman, U. (1992). Studying students studying calculus: A look at the lives of minority mathematics students in college. *College Mathematics Journal,* 362–372.

Trumbore, A. (2014). Rules of engagement: Strategies to increase online engagement at scale. *Change: The Magazine of Higher Learning, 48*(1), 38–45.

Walton, G. M., Cohen, G. L., Cwir, D., & Spencer, S. J. (2012). Mere belonging: the power of social connections. *Journal of Personality and Social Psychology, 102*(3), 513.

Zimmerman, B. J. (2002). Becoming a self-regulated learner: An overview. *Theory into Practice, 41*(2), 64–70.

8

MOOCS, COPYRIGHT, AND THE MANY MEANINGS OF "OPEN"

Samantha Bernstein

Massive open online courses (MOOCs) have been the source of much controversy in higher education. They raise some novel legal issues, and present an interesting challenge in the areas of intellectual property (IP) and oversight. MOOCs are distinguishable from traditional and distance learning courses in a number of ways. First, students do not enroll in a university when they enroll in a MOOC— completion of a MOOC is rarely if ever accompanied by official college credit. Second, most MOOC providers operate independently of federal funding, and students require no financial assistance to participate in the course. As a result, MOOCs tend to fall outside of the regulatory framework of U.S. Higher Education (Goldstein & Ferenbach, 2013). Given the variety of contracts, policies, and laws undergirding educational innovations like MOOCs, it will be useful for universities to understand the ambiguities in the law, and the rights of all affected parties.

Though every letter of the acronym is arguably negotiable, this chapter is concerned primarily with the "open" in MOOCs, and the controversy that this word triggers in the world of educational technology (Plourde, 2013). In the following chapter, I explore the commonly cited legal issues raised by MOOCs in an attempt to flesh out the nuanced distinctions between MOOCs and other methods of course delivery. First, I provide a foundational discussion of the development of MOOCs to explore the legal backdrop against which they arose. Next, I consider copyright and the open license—an essential tool in many recent educational innovations. Following, I examine a sample of legal issues and tensions from the perspective of the university, faculty, and students, and I conclude with the implications of MOOCs for the global society.

MOOC Foundations

MOOCs are currently the most visible online learning enterprise in higher education, but they arose out of a lengthy tradition of distance learning. Before the internet, correspondence courses were delivered through radio. "Colleges of the air" swept the United States in the 1920s and 30s, with students registering and completing assignments by mail (Matt & Fernandez, 2013). Projects such as the UK's Open University offered distance learning degrees as early as the 1970s (Open University, 2014). Much like MOOCs, advocates of these early projects hoped that distance learning would promote equity by reaching populations who would not otherwise have access to higher education.

cMOOCs

The term "MOOC" was created to describe a very different phenomenon from that which is making headlines in 2014. There are two categories of MOOCs: "c" and "x." The first MOOC, entitled "Connectivism and Connective Knowledge," was developed in 2008 by George Siemens and Stephen Downes at the University of Manitoba, as an experiment in networking pedagogy. In addition to the fee paying residential students who registered for credit, an additional 2,300 non-university students enrolled in the course for free. This MOOC, and others like it, are now called "cMOOCs," the "c" deriving from connectivism, the theory upon which the early MOOCs were based.

cMOOCs are defined by two distinct pedagogical characteristics. First, learning occurs through a mutual construction of knowledge, which encourages dialogue, communication, and an open approach to course content. Second, learning through cMOOCs is inherently social. Student networks are encouraged to persist beyond the course in order to facilitate learning (Anderson & Dron, 2011). cMOOCs were born out of the open educational resources (OER)[1] movement, which promotes equity and the removal of financial and legal barriers to educational access through the use of open licensing. cMOOCs are distributed, in the sense that materials do not exist in a central website, and no new content is created for the course. All materials are open—either in the public domain, or OER. According to Siemens (2011), cMOOCs

> are about shared ownership and transparency. An open course starts as a shell with the instructor providing links, articles, and activities. From there, learners take course content and massage it, enhance it, extend it, clarify it, question it, and improve it.

xMOOCs

Three years after the first MOOC launched, Sebastian Thrun and Peter Norvig ushered in a new generation of MOOCs with their 2011 Stanford course,

"Introduction to Artificial Intelligence," (AI) for which 160,000 students enrolled from 209 countries (Yeager, Hurley-Dasgupta, & Bliss, 2013; Norvig, 2012). The course was comprised of short videos between two and six minutes, including quizzes and weekly homework assignments. Approximately 20,000 students finished the AI course and received a certificate of completion. Public interest was piqued, and the MOOC movement gained further traction after the founding of tech start-ups (MOOC providers) offering assistance to universities who wished to create their own.

After the success of the AI MOOC, Thrun left Stanford to found Udacity, a for-profit MOOC provider offering primarily STEM courses through collaborations with Google, Microsoft, and other tech-based organizations and community colleges. Coursera was founded in 2012 by Stanford professors Daphne Koller and Andrew Ng, and Harvard and MIT joined forces to create the non-profit, edX, which partners with prestigious universities like UC Berkeley, Tufts, and Georgetown. Udacity, Coursera, and edX are three of the most popular providers of "xMOOCs" operating today. Termed "xMOOCs" due to the nature of the courses as "eXtended" from the core offerings of residential universities, these MOOCs are often co-developed by established universities who partner with the MOOC provider, to offer adapted versions of an existing university course.

Though the following analysis deals primarily with xMOOCs, the pedagogical distinction described here is fundamental to a discussion of MOOCs law because the two models ("c" and "x") trigger different meanings of ownership. Where cMOOCs require flexibility of content in order to perpetuate social constructions of knowledge, the traditional "sage on the stage" pedagogical model used in xMOOCs is premised on a single truth, with clearly delineated boundaries that conform more easily to fixed categories in the law governing knowledge ownership.

Copyright and the Open License

"Open" can mean many things, but in the context of MOOCs, three definitions are particularly relevant: open can mean (1) free, as in *gratis*, or at no cost; (2) open to all who wish to participate; or (3) lacking legal restrictions. Most MOOCs conform with (1) and (2), but xMOOCs often place legal restrictions on video and course content. Coursera, Udacity, and edX, among other xMOOC providers, utilize various forms of licensing to restrict certain types of use. Licensing and copyright are the source of most MOOC law issues, prompting one of the most salient questions from a legal perspective: who owns a MOOC?

The key legal feature distinguishing cMOOCs and xMOOCs is the open license. Facilitated through organizations like Creative Commons, the touchstone of the open license is that no single person "owns" the resource in the traditional sense of ownership. Creators of a knowledge resource retain copyright over content, but sacrifice control over its use and dissemination. Materials can be accessed and repurposed for educational purposes, free of charge, and in exchange for this access, users need only credit the creator, and refrain from commercial use of the content. The open license signifies the implicit agreement by creators that no person should be excluded from accessing the resources.

Most of the new xMOOCs are free to access, but not openly licensed, meaning that restrictions on MOOC content prevent faculty and users from sharing, reusing, and remixing content. For instance, Coursera's terms of service state that:

> Coursera grants you a personal, non-exclusive, non-transferable license to access and use the Sites. You may download material from the Sites only for your own personal, non-commercial use. You may *not* otherwise copy, reproduce, retransmit, distribute, publish, commercially exploit or otherwise transfer any material, nor may you modify or create derivatives works of the material. The burden of determining that your use of any information, software or any other content on the Site is permissible rests with you.
>
> (Coursera, 2014, emphasis added)

Coursera users are granted only rights of access and personal use, but are not permitted to modify, reproduce, or redistribute the content they use. Though Udacity content is published under a Creative Commons license, that particular license (Creative Commons Attribution-NonCommercial-NoDerivs 3.0) is more restrictive than other forms. That license grants to users rights of access, personal use, and the right to share materials, but users are prohibited from adapting or remixing materials, or creating derivative works (Carr, 2013).

Property rights over knowledge raise large-scale societal questions for governments, rights holders, and the public (Peters, 2003). Broad IP rights—those which accrue overwhelmingly in favor of the copyright holder—signal a danger of market monopolization. On the other hand, permissive IP rights permitting open access to the public effectively border on intellectual piracy, and risk the diminution of knowledge supply by removing incentives for the knowledge producer. Effective intellectual property systems must therefore engage in a balancing act between incentivizing knowledge creation, and restricting societal access to it (Stiglitz, 1999).

Use restrictions on MOOC content benefit MOOC providers by leaving open the possibility for of a multitude of revenue models, which is one aspect of xMOOCs that remains unsettled. When asked in a Keynote address about Coursera's restrictive terms of use, co-founder Andrew Ng (2013) responded that he believed licensing would play a substantial role in creating a sustainable business model—a necessity if Coursera is to continue providing free education to students around the world. As discussed in other chapters of this book, if MOOCs are to remain free to students, providers will have to experiment with models other than tuition-based revenue, and find alternative ways of exploiting this innovative course delivery system.

The Problems

Despite the variety and complexity of MOOC models and their licensing features, problems may arise as a result of competing interests of the various parties involved in a MOOC endeavor. In order to host an xMOOC, universities must partner with a provider, and allocate rights of use, ownership, and dissemination through contracts. Faculty members develop the content with financial support from the university, and through MOOC participation, users contribute their individual work in public forums. Universities, faculty, and students may all assert rights to access, use, disseminate, or own MOOCs. What follows is a discussion of the potential problems and tensions raised by this muddle of interests, and how the laws and policies governing traditional higher education either may or may not apply.

What Can Be Included in a MOOC?

Most written works used in educational materials are protected by U.S. Copyright law. These works can be licensed to a university for a fee, and provided to enrolled students for educational purposes. Explicit exceptions exist for educational purposes that allow instructors to use protected works in their course content. MOOCs are unique in that participating students are not necessarily enrolled in the host university, and copyright laws and exceptions do not apply in the same way as they would in a traditional university course.

The fair use doctrine in U.S. Copyright law (17 U.S.C. § 107, 1976) allows for the use of copyrighted material without permission or payment, when the benefit to society is greater than the damage to the copyright holder (American University School of Communication, 2009). No special licenses are required in order to benefit from fair use in a traditional face-to-face classroom, in furtherance of an educational mission. Factors to consider in determining whether fair use applies include whether the work will be employed in a commercial or for-profit endeavor (Kaplin & Lee, 2007), and the size and geographic scope of the MOOC offering. In spite of explicit educational exceptions to the Copyright Act, MOOC creators (often faculty members) may be unable to claim fair use of third party licensed material, depending on the nature of the MOOC.

> Some publishers, museums, and other content owners are asking extra-ordinarily high prices or refusing to license for MOOC teaching, citing the for-profit nature of the platforms as well as the unprecedented scale. Others are simply not responding to these requests. Campus counsel at one library has advised that fair use is not an option in the context of MOOCs.
>
> (Butler, 2012, p. 2)

This may mean that materials used in the MOOC must either belong to the MOOC creator or university, reside in the public domain, or be openly licensed. Many of the issues of concern to faculty members are also relevant to the university, as institutions may be liable for any unlawful acts of their employees. For this reason, prior to hosting a MOOC, universities should ensure that all third party content used is properly licensed, or in the public domain.

MOOC Provider Contracts

The relationship between MOOC providers and the university is governed by contract. As no two institutions are identical, every MOOC contract will differ to some degree, depending on the substance of negotiations between the parties, and the needs and values of the particular university. In terms of copyright, MOOC providers rarely seek ownership rights over course content, but merely rights to distribute and use the content (Wessel, 2013). However, Wessel (2013) suggests that, as business models evolve, some providers have started to seek additional rights from institutions, including accreditation, resale rights, and the rights to produce textbooks and other course materials. Although there is no formula for contract negotiations, non-exclusive agreements may be preferable for the university because they allow for greater flexibility. Additionally, the terms of a MOOC provider contract often have implications for the rights of both faculty MOOC-creators and student MOOC-users, which differ from the rights conferred by typical university policies. These unique features are discussed in greater detail below.

Copyright Tensions between Faculty and the University

A debate has gained momentum in the academic community over the ownership rights of faculty members to works created in the course of employment with a university. The Bayh-Dole Act of 1980 is a federal law that conferred ownership rights to universities for faculty discoveries made during the course of research under government grants (Slaughter & Rhoades, 2010). Universities created specific policies outlining the various rights and responsibilities of faculty members and the institution, and delineating how proceeds would be divided in the event of a discovery. In the 1980s and 1990s, these policies began to include copyright in addition to patents, and, at present, every research university in the U.S. has a policy in place governing faculty rights to academic work.

The American Association of University Professors (AAUP) (2000) advised in its statement on distance learning that absent a specific agreement with the university, faculty members are entitled to ownership of the intellectual property they create. Though the "Work Made for Hire" doctrine (1976) of the U.S. Copyright Act contains a default provision in favor of employer ownership, the courts have recognized an academic exception to this provision based on the unique aspects of academic work, including academic freedom, faculty autonomy, and the university's desire to attract and retain the most productive faculty (Porter, 2013). Recently, the AAUP has spoken out about the copyright debate in higher education. Though patent ownership has been a controversial topic for many years, universities have generally left faculty copyright of their courses and research alone (Schmidt, 2013). However, given the profit-generating potential of MOOCS, many universities have begun to assert rights to their faculty members' online courses.

Cary Nelson, former president of the AAUP, asserts that university claims to MOOCs and other online courses will open the floodgates, with universities expropriating the research of faculty, leaving the academic profession in ruin. If universities assert rights to online courses, there is nothing to stop them from claiming traditional course materials or research publications. In that event, "'being a professor will no longer be a professional career or a professional identity,' and faculty members will instead essentially find themselves working in 'a service industry'" (Schmidt, 2013).

Though universities are free to develop their copyright policies and allocate rights how they deem appropriate, it is important for policy-makers to understand the history of intellectual property in the academic community, so as to avoid making decisions that may deter the best and the brightest faculty members, or result in a lawsuit. As university resources are used in the creation of MOOC courses, institutions have a strong financial interest in the content developed by faculty. Despite the academic exception to the Copyright Act, the university may claim ownership of a course in instances where a faculty member utilized significant university resources in its creation, was specifically commissioned by the university, or where multiple university personnel were involved in its development (Porter, 2013). Porter suggests that most MOOCs will likely fall in this category because universities invest considerable financial resources in faculty members to develop MOOCs, including grants, summer money, research leaves, and sabbaticals.

User Rights in MOOCs

Unlike MOOC users, traditional university students are entitled to certain rights and protections under the law by virtue of their enrollment in accredited educational institutions. Among these are the right to privacy under the Family Educational Rights and Privacy Act (1974) (FERPA), and copyright to student work (Finkel, 2013).

MOOC providers make no secret of the fact that they collect personally identifiable information from enrolled users, and engage in data mining for various purposes. Among them, providers use information in educational research for the purpose of improving future course delivery, and to share it with other companies for marketing purposes. The following is provided in the privacy policy available on the Coursera (2014) website:

Communications with Coursera Business Partners. We may share your Personally Identifiable Information with University partners and other business partners of Coursera so that Coursera University partners and other business partners may share information about their products and services that may be of interest to you.

Research. We may share general course data (including quiz or assignment submissions, grades, and forum discussions), information about your activity on our Site, and demographic data from surveys operated by us with our University partners and other business partners so that our University partners and other business partners may use the data for research related to online education.

FERPA is intended to protect the confidentiality of students' educational data. In a typical university setting, the gathered data referenced above is private, and higher education institutions are prohibited by law from sharing it with anyone but the student unless certain exceptions apply.[2] These exceptions include the right of school officials to examine documents where they have a "legitimate educational interest," or to comply with a court subpoena. The purpose of FERPA is to protect the student from dissemination of personal educational information to third parties, but these provisions apply only to educational or authorized agencies who receive federal funding to provide educational services to students.

In addition to quizzes, forum postings, and grade performance, MOOC providers collect information for the purpose of analytics, including social media profiles, time logged in on Facebook while in class, downloads, uploads, and Wikipedia visits (Watters, 2013). According to Coursera co-founder Daphne Koller, this information allows analysts to study learning in ways never before explored. In a presentation to the University of Southern California's Rossier School of Education, Koller displayed a graph along a timeline showing weekly "pulses" of activity, equating to traffic on the Coursera website occurring immediately before homework deadlines. Additionally, data collected by Coursera can be used to evaluate the notoriously high attrition rates attributed to MOOCs and to determine, based on initial surveys, which types of users will be more likely to successfully complete a course. Though the idea of student data used in furtherance of educational improvement and the public good is an intriguing one, it is also fairly easy to imagine some inequitable uses for the results of those surveys, such as barriers to enrollment.

A less frequently discussed issue for MOOC users is ownership of content contributed to the course. Students in traditional universities hold copyright over the work they produce for courses, including homework, exams, and research papers, but this issue is much less clear in the MOOC arena (Porter, 2013).The Coursera privacy policy advises students to "keep in mind that information you post or make available in Forums will be publicly available" (Coursera, 2014). Its terms of use require that students "grant Coursera and the Participating

Institutions a fully transferable, worldwide, perpetual, royalty-free and non-exclusive license to use, distribute, sublicense, reproduce, modify, adapt, publicly perform and publicly display" user content. Where the user-generated content is comprised of answers to short quizzes and forum postings, the issue of ownership is less concerning than that of cMOOCs. Since student writings are integral to the foundation of the cMOOC, it is unclear whether students are considered content creators, and therefore copyright holders of the works they contribute (Rodriguez, 2013).

Looking Ahead

The cost of knowledge is a contentious and ongoing debate, which raises ethical questions of basic human rights. Many argue that the price tag of knowledge should not be such that it inhibits educational access (Johan Lor & Britz, 2005; Stiglitz, 1999). Though advocates of the open education movement might disagree with the xMOOC licensing models, if courses are offered for free around the world to anyone with an internet connection, does it matter that they cannot be freely shared or adapted? The answer to this question is largely subjective, depending on one's own beliefs about pedagogy and the purposes of education.

Because MOOCs are a relatively new phenomenon, there is little guidance in the form of statutory or case law explicitly addressing the legal issues discussed above. Legal analysis and planning for universities requires much speculation based on current copyright law and how past case law might apply to MOOCs. Regardless of how these various tensions are resolved, it is clear that MOOCs raise a number of large-scale issues with the potential to drastically change the role of the faculty member and the student in higher education.

Much of the mainstream controversy relating to MOOCs is reminiscent of apocalyptic prophecies of the collapse of traditional higher education. In a world of MOOCs, far from *in loco parentis*, students are consumers and data points whose contributions aid in the refinement of the educational machine. The intellectual work product of faculty members resides with the university, resulting in the demise of tenure and the academic profession. Though the future of higher education is uncertain, the MOOC foray into the mainstream has stimulated important discussions about student access, and the cost of higher education. Answers to the problems of access may not lie with MOOCs, but innovations like these may be stepping stones to workable solutions, and are therefore certainly worth watching.

Notes

1   OERs are defined as teaching, learning, or research materials that are in the public domain or released with an open IP license (Organization for Economic Cooperation and Development, 2007).
2   See Section 34 C.F.R. §99.31.

References

AAUP (2000). Faculty Rights and Responsibilities in Distance Learning. www.aaup.org/faculty-rights-and-responsibilities-distance-learning-2000

American University School of Communication (2009). Code of Best Practices in Fair Use for OpenCourseWare. *Center for Social Media.* www.cmsimpact.org/sites/default/files/10-305-OCW-Oct29.pdf

Anderson, T. & Dron, J. (2011). "Three Generations of Distance Education Pedagogy." *International Review of Research in Open and Distance Learning,* 12(3).

Bayh-Dole Act (1980). Pub. L. No. 65–517.

Butler, B. (2012). "Issue Brief: Massive Open Online Courses: Legal and Policy Issues for Research Libraries." *Association of Research Libraries,* 22.

Carr, D. F. (2013). Udacity Hedges on Open Licensing for MOOCs. *Information Week.* www.informationweek.com/education/online-learning/udacity-hedges-on-open-licensing-for-moo/240160183

Coursera (2014). Coursera Privacy Policy. www.coursera.org/about/privacy

Family Educational Rights and Privacy Act (1974). 34 C.F.R. Part 99.

Finkel, E. (2013). Data Mining the MOOCs. *University Business.* www.universitybusiness.com/article/data-mining-moocs

Goldstein, M. & Ferenbach, G. (2013). Legal and Regulatory Aspects of MOOC Mania. *University Business.* www.universitybusiness.com/article/legal-and-regulatory-aspects-mooc-mania

Johan Lor, P., & Britz, J. (2005). Knowledge Production from an African Perspective: International Information Flows and Intellectual Property. *The International Information & Library Review,* 37(2), 61–76.

Kaplin, W. & Lee, B. (2007). *The Law of Higher Education.* Fourth Edition. Jossey-Bass: San Francisco, CA.

Matt, S. & Fernandez, L. (2013). Before MOOCs, 'Colleges of the Air.' *The Chronicle of Higher Education.*

Norvig, P. (2012). The 100,000 Student Classroom. Ted Talk. www.ted.com/talks/peter_norvig_the_100_000_student_classroom.html

Organization for Economic Cooperation and Development (2007). *Giving Knowledge for Free: The Emergence of Open Educational Resources.* OECD.

Open University (2014). Open University United Kingdom. www.open.ac.uk/research projects/historyofou/story/first-students-and-first-graduates

Ng, A. (2013). *Keynote Pairing.* Presentation via Skype at the Open Education Conference. Park City, UT.

Peters, M. (2003). Classical Political Economy and the Role of Universities in the New Knowledge Economy. *Globalisation, Societies and Education,* 1(2), 153–168.

Plourde, M. (2013). Every Letter is Negotiable. http://edtechdigest.wordpress.com/2013/11/14/trends-mooc-negotiable/

Porter, J. (2013). MOOCs, "Courses," and the Question of Faculty and Student Copyrights. *The CCCC-IP Annual: Top Intellectual Property Developments of 2012.* pp. 2–18. Intellectual property Caucus of the Conference on College Composition and Communication.

Rodriguez, O. (2013). The Concept of Openness Behind c and x-MOOCs (Massive Open Online Courses). *Open Praxis,* 5(1).

Schmidt, P. (2013). AAUP Sees MOOCs as Spawning New Threats to Professors' Intellectual Property. http://chronicle.com/article/AAUP-Sees-MOOCs-as-Spawning/139743/

Siemens, G. (2011). Stanford AI MOOC: Let's Try Transparency. *Elearnspace*. www.elearnspace.org/blog/2011/09/09/stanford-ai-mooc-lets-try-transparency/

Slaughter, S. & Rhoades, G. (2010). The Social Construction of Copyright Ethics and Values. *Science and Engineering Ethics*, 16(2), pp. 263–293.

Stiglitz, J. (1999). Knowledge as a Global Public Good. In I. Kaul, I. Grunberg, & M. Stern (Eds.), *Global Public Goods* (pp. 308–325). New York: Oxford University Press.

U.S. Copyright Act (1976). 17 U.S.C. § 107. Fair Use.

Watters, A. (2013). Student Data is the New Oil. MOOCs, Metaphor, and Money. http://hackeducation.com/2013/10/17/student-data-is-the-new-oil/

Wessel, M. (2013). Legal Issues in MOOCs. *Educause*. https://net.educause.edu/ir/library/pdf/LIVE1319S.pdf

Yeager, C., Hurley-Dasgupta, B., & Bliss, C. A. (2013). cMOOCs and Global Learning: An Authentic Alternative. *Journal of Asynchronous Learning Networks*, 17(2).

9

EDUCATING EDUCATORS

Designing MOOCs for Professional Learning[1]

Glenn M. Kleiman, Mary Ann Wolf, and David Frye

Introduction

We have long been engaged in providing professional learning opportunities for educators, including K-12 teachers, school and district leaders, college of education faculty, and state department of education staff. Our work over two decades has led us to continuously explore variations of face-to-face, online, and blended professional learning experiences as both the available technologies and the technological fluency of our audiences advanced. The advent of MOOCs has led us to consider their potential to help education professionals advance their expertise and improve their professional practices. This chapter describes the first year of our efforts, the design principles underlying our work, lessons learned, and future directions of what we call *MOOC-Eds*—Massive Open Online Courses for Educators.

The Need for MOOCs for Educators (MOOC-Eds)

The need for large-scale, widely accessible, cost-effective professional development opportunities for educators is very clear. K-12 education is undergoing rapid changes driven by:

- new curriculum standards and student assessments;
- the importance of digital literacies and the 4 Cs (critical thinking, communications, collaboration, and creativity) in preparing students to be college, career, and citizenship ready;

- increased use of data systems to inform instructional, programmatic, and policy decisions;
- teacher evaluation systems that use student learning gains to assess the *value added* by each teacher; and
- technologies to enhance teaching, learning, assessment, communications, and school management.

In addition, schools need to address the increased diversity of student populations and the economic constraints leading to larger class sizes, fewer resources, and the need to make education more productive and cost-effective.

These changes impact a large education workforce. The National Center for Educational Statistics reports that there were 3.7 million full-time-equivalent K-12 school teachers in fall 2012. Of these, 3.3 million were in public schools and 0.4 million were in private schools. The public school teachers were distributed across almost 100,000 schools in almost 18,000 districts, with more than 200,000 administrators. Private schools added an additional 50,000 administrators (National Center for Education Statistics, 2014, http://nces.ed.gov/programs/digest/d12/index.asp).

To address these changes, both teachers and administrators require opportunities to update their own knowledge, skills, and practices through professional development. The Friday Institute began a program that focuses on the potential for MOOC-Eds to address these needs by bringing together expertise in several key areas:

- design of technology-enabled professional development for educators;
- technology platforms that can enhance online learning and online communities of practice;
- implementing and delivering face-to-face, online, and blended professional development programs; and
- conducting research on online teaching, learning, and professional communities.

In 2013, the Friday Institute twice offered a MOOC-Ed on *Planning for the Digital Learning Transition in K-12 Schools*, which is the primary basis for this chapter. We are currently deploying another MOOC-Ed for instructional coaches, instructional technology facilitators, media specialists, and others who guide teachers in incorporating digital learning into their classrooms. We are also developing MOOC-Eds for teachers and teacher educators on implementing the Common Core Mathematics and English Language Arts Standards and on learning differences and personalization in K-12 education. These MOOC-Eds provide the basis for an active and growing research program. Current information about our work is always available at www.mooc-ed.org.

Principles of Effective Professional Development for Educators

Traditionally, K-12 professional development consists of a few days per year when districts release educators from their teaching or administrative responsibilities to attend workshops. Typically, these workshops provide information through "sit and listen" presentations that, as research repeatedly demonstrates, may increase awareness of changing expectations, but do not lead to changes in educational practices or improvements in student achievement. The National Staff Development Council/Learning Forward (Darling-Hammond, Wei, Richardson, & Orphanos, 2009) reports "nearly half of all U.S. teachers are dissatisfied with their opportunities for professional development." A significant body of research (summarized by Wei, Darling-Hammond, & Adamson, 2010) has established that professional development for educators is most effective in improving teaching practices and student achievement when it:

- fosters a deepening of subject-matter knowledge, a greater understanding of learning, and a greater appreciation of students' needs;
- centers around the critical activities of teaching and learning—planning lessons, evaluating student work, developing curriculum, improving classroom practices, and increasing student learning;
- builds on investigations of practice through cases that involve specific problems of practice, questions, analysis, reflection, and substantial professional discourse;
- provides educators with opportunities to learn in the way they will be expected to teach;
- is personalized to address the specific professional learning needs of each individual;
- values and cultivates a culture of collegiality, involving knowledge and experience sharing among educators; and,
- is sustained, intensive, and continuously woven into the everyday fabric of the profession, through modeling, coaching, and collaborations.

While the need for large scale educator professional development is clear and the principles of effective programs well established, the resources available to meet this critical need are limited and have been declining in many states and districts. Using traditional professional development approaches is far too costly, cannot provide sufficient learning opportunities when and where educators need them, and is of limited effectiveness even for those educators they can reach. New approaches are required, approaches that embody the principles of effective professional development and are scalable, accessible, and flexible to meet the needs of many educators.

MOOC-Ed Design Principles

Our approach differs from most other MOOCs in that it is designed in accordance with the research-based principles of effective professional development ((Darling-Hammond, Wei, Richardson, & Orphanos, 2009) and online learning (iNACOL, 2011), which we incorporate into four major design principles for MOOC-Eds:

*   *Self-directed learning,* so that participants are encouraged to personalize their own professional learning goals and identify them at the beginning of the MOOC-Ed, select among a rich array of resources, and decide whether, when, and how to engage in discussions and activities to further their own learning and meet their goals.
*   *Peer supported learning,* so that educators support each other through engagement in online discussions, peer reviews of projects, ratings of posted ideas, and crowdsourcing of lessons learned; while those working in local teams also support each other by working on the MOOC-Ed activities in collaboration with local colleagues.
*   *Case study and project-based approaches* to build upon examples of best practices while centering participants' work on critical problems of practice and data-informed decision-making in their own classrooms, schools, or districts.
*   *Designed for integration into blended learning programs* to maximize the potential to integrate MOOC-Eds within larger scale professional development programs that provide face-to-face and hands-on activities, individual coaching, local professional learning communities, and other professional learning experiences.

From Design Principles to the Digital Learning Transition MOOC-Ed

The Digital Learning Transition (DLT), offered in collaboration with the Alliance for Excellent Education (the Alliance), was our first MOOC-Ed based on these design principles. It is intended for K-12 school and district leaders and others involved in planning and implementing digital learning initiatives. We have now offered the DLT MOOC-Ed twice, and we plan to offer it during the winter semester each year moving forward. The goals for participants are:

1.   Understand the impact of technology and the global information age on both *what* students need to learn and *how* learning can take place.
2.   Explore best practices and lessons learned from schools and districts that have digital learning transitions well underway.
3.   Develop a set of digital learning goals for your own school or district.
4.   Consider the elements of a successful digital learning transition and effective strategies for addressing each element.

5.   Examine processes and tools that help support planning, implementing, and evaluating a digital learning transition.
6.   Develop an action plan to meet your school or district digital learning transition goals.
7.   Contribute to the learning of others who participate in the course.

The DLT MOOC-Ed was organized around the Digital Learning Transition Planning Framework. Based on the work of the Alliance's Project 24 and the Friday Institute's Digital Learning Collaborative, this framework is designed to help educators plan digital learning initiatives to meet district and school goals. As shown in Figure 9.1, the framework incorporates four cyclical processes—vision, plan, implement, and assess—and seven key elements—curriculum and instruction, use of time, technology, and instruction, data and assessment,

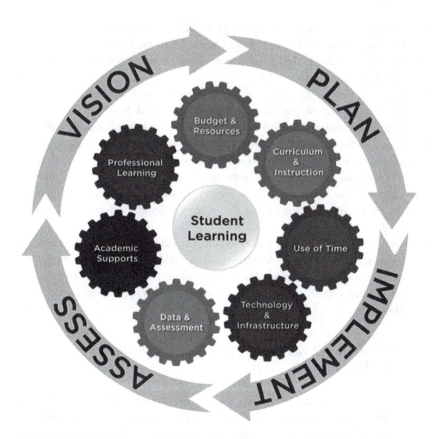

FIGURE 9.1 Digital Learning Initiative Planning Framework

Source: Image courtesy of the Alliance for Excellent Education and the Friday Institute for Educational Innovation.

academic supports, professional learning, and budget and resources—that must be addressed for a K-12 digital learning initiative to successfully improve student learning. The Alliance's Project 24 provides a self-assessment to help districts and schools assess their digital learning readiness, which was incorporated into the MOOC-Ed, along with selected Project 24 webinars, blogs, and other resources.

The DLT MOOC-Ed contains eight units divided into two parts, with each unit planned for one week. The course outline is shown below:

Digital Learning Transition MOOC-Ed Course Outline

Part I: Where Are We Heading? Goals for the Digital Learning Transition.

- *Unit 1: Envisioning Schools in the Year 2020.* Participants further their thinking about the vision for the Digital Learning Transition in their schools and their ability to communicate that vision to multiple stakeholder groups.
- *Unit 2: Changing the Culture of Teaching and Learning.* This unit focuses on the impact of digital learning on classroom practices and on expanding students' opportunities to learn beyond the classroom walls.
- *Unit 3: School and District Digital Learning Transitions.* Using a case study approach, participants turn to case studies of schools and districts that have digital learning transitions well underway. Participants also complete the first part of their project on their digital learning goals for their school or district and the major challenges in reaching those goals.
- *Unit 4: Wrap Up of Part I.* Participants provide constructive feedback to each other on their recommendations of digital learning goals for their schools and districts. They also complete the Part I discussions, crowdsource the most important lessons learned and complete a survey about the DLT MOOC-Ed.

Part II: How Do We Get There? Planning for a Digital Learning Transition.

- *Unit 5: Preparing and Supporting Teachers and Administrators in the Digital Learning Transition.* Many digital learning initiatives have not been successful because they focused on the technology infrastructure without sufficient attention to the human infrastructure—the teachers and administrators who need to learn and update their practices. In this unit, participants focus on planning professional development, coaching and other supports for teachers and administrators.

- *Unit 6: Planning for the DLT Elements.* Prior units addressed the framework elements of curriculum and instruction (Unit 2) and professional learning (Unit 5). In this unit, participants explore the remaining elements from the planning framework into three topic areas: (1) *Providing the Technology Tools*; (2) *Beyond the School Walls and Schedules*; and (3) *Making Informed Instructional Decisions.* Each participant selects one of these topic areas to focus on, learning about innovative strategies, assessing the current status in their school or district and planning how to move things forward.
- *Unit 7: Leading a Successful Digital Learning Initiative.* Participants learn about effective strategies for distributed, team-based leadership, then review and consider recommendations for their local leadership structure and approach. Participants also complete and submit their projects, adding strategies and actions steps to their goals and challenges.
- *Session 8: Wrap Up and Next Steps.* Participants provide constructive feedback about each other's strategies and action plans. They also crowdsource major lessons learned about professional learning, leadership and action planning that inform their planning of their local initiatives. To complete the unit, they provide feedback about the MOOC-Ed experience and recommendations for future MOOC-Eds.

Prior to the start of the MOOC-Ed, registrants completed a survey that provides information about their goals and demographics. Participants could take an optional *School and District Digital Learning Readiness Self-Assessment*, developed by the Metiri Group for the Alliance for Excellent Education's Project 24 initiative, and receive a detailed report about their school's or district's digital learning readiness for each of the seven elements in the framework. The MOOC-Ed provided opportunities for participants to use the data to inform their planning.

Each unit was introduced by brief text with essential questions and a short (4–8 minute) video in which Mary Ann Wolf and Glenn Kleiman, the course developers, introduced the content and expectations for the unit. Figure 9.2 shows an example page from the DLT MOOC-Ed, the introductory page to Unit 2 on *Changing the Culture of Teaching and Learning*, with the unit introductory video presentation in process.

Participants were invited to select options such as those along the left side of Figure 9.2 to move through each unit's activities in any order they choose:

- *Review core resources* and, for some units, additional recommended resources, with both video and print resources typically provided in each.

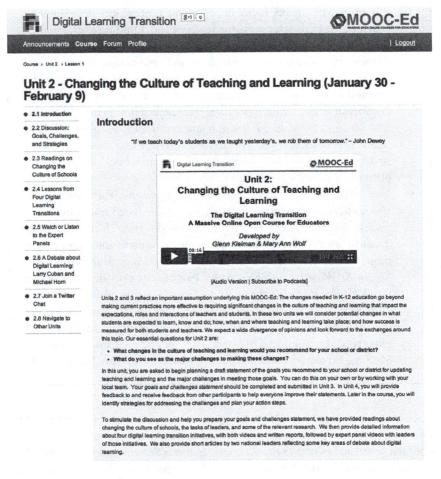

FIGURE 9.2 Example page from the DLT MOOC-Ed

Source: Image courtesy of The Friday Institute for Educational Innovation.

- *Participate in discussions about the unit content.* The facilitators seeded the discussion for each unit, and participants could respond to the initial discussion topics and initiate new ones. Participants could also directly address prior comments through a "quote" option, and tag others' postings (selecting from *agree, disagree* or *insightful* tags).
- *Learn from panels of national experts* from schools, districts, and other organizations, specifically selected for their expertise in the content for each unit. In recorded Google Hangout discussions that were then available throughout the remainder of the course, expert panelist(s) addressed key issues relevant to the unit.

- *Engage in planning projects and then provide and receive peer feedback* about their plans. Participants, working either individually or in teams, were invited to submit their recommended digital learning goals and challenges for their school or district in unit and then their recommended strategies and actions steps for addressing the goals in Unit 7. In units 4 and 8, participants were invited to review and provide constructive feedback on each other's plans.
- *Crowdsource the most important ideas and valuable strategies* to incorporate into school and district plans. Participants were also asked to select which resources were most valuable and recommend additional resources for their peers, which were compiled into a set of participant suggested resources.
- *Complete surveys about the DLT MOOC-Ed* at the midpoint and end of the course, and provide comments about the MOOC-Ed and recommendations for future ones.

We integrated several technology platforms to support the video presentations, resources, and interactions in the MOOC-Ed. Google Course Builder running on the Google App Engine provided the overall structure for organizing the MOOC-Ed and presenting information. We integrated Vanilla Forums with Course Builder to provide the discussion forum functions, along with Survey Gizmo for crowdsourcing and other surveys. Google Hangouts was used to record the expert panels and Vimeo was used to make the course-developed videos available.

DLT MOOC-Ed Data Sources

MOOC-Eds are very new, and provide an opportunity to explore many questions about what professional learning purposes they can serve and how they can best be designed and implemented. For the DLT MOOC-Ed, these data include:

- user demographics, role, level of education and experience, goals for participating, and other information collected during a required pre-registration survey;
- overall web analytics of visitors, visits, visit duration, pages viewed, from where, using what technology, and other data, for any range of days during the course;
- detailed "click logs" of each user's access to each unit in the course site, the specific pages accessed, and time spent on each page;
- discussion forum views, discussions started, and comments within discussions for each unit by each participant;
- discussion forum content, which can be subjected to various forms of discourse analyses;
- projects submitted and reviews of projects submitted by each participant;
- total views and average time viewing for each of the videos created for the course and made available through our Vimeo site;

- user ratings of each of the course resources and suggestions for additional resources from crowdsourcing activities embedded in the course;
- mid-point and end of course survey asking participants to rate the value of the course overall and of specific elements of the course; and
- open-ended responses from participants, in both the surveys and the discussions, about what value they found in the course and how it can be improved.

We are exploring multiple analyses of these data to describe how participants engage in the DLT MOOC-Ed to validate and refine our design principles and to develop hypotheses and design experiments for further research. This work is constantly developing, so this chapter provides a status report and working ideas based on our first year of work with MOOC-Eds, not summative findings or definitive conclusions. First we present a summary of key findings, followed by general findings about the registrants in the two DLT MOOC-Eds (DLT1 and DLT2) and their participation in the course, and then we examine data relevant to each of the design principles. The detailed data is from DLT2 only, since we have more analytics data available from that course.

Summary of Key Findings

- Findings from our early MOOC-Eds show that educators from around the U.S. and around the world are interested in this type of professional development, with registrants from all U.S. states and 90 countries representing many types of schools, roles within schools, and levels of experience. The participants had a variety of goals for taking the course, such as preparing to lead change in their school or district, understanding the potential of digital learning, experiencing a MOOC, and improving their own classroom teaching. This finding highlights the need to design MOOC-Eds to address the diverse needs of large national and international groups of participants.
- A substantial number of participants actively engaged in the course, as measured by course visits, page views, video views, discussion forum postings and views, and time on the course site. However, only about 50 percent of those who registered participated in the first unit and there is an ongoing decline in the number of participants across units. We are more concerned about whether participants met their own professional learning goals than in whether they "completed" the courses, but in the second DLT MOOC-Ed, 12.2 percent of those who participated in the first unit completed the course. The data are broadly consistent with findings from other MOOCs and raise questions about how to increase ongoing engagement in MOOC-Eds. It also points to the importance of distinguishing among *registrants*, *starting participants* and *ongoing participants* to accurately convey the scale of impact of MOOCs.

- While the MOOC-Eds are presented in weekly units, we find that at any given week after the first, many participants are still engaged in prior units. For example, during Week 5, about 50 percent of the clicks in the MOOC-Ed site were on units 1–4. This finding points to the need to build flexibility into MOOC-Ed course schedules, while also enabling participants to engage in peer-supported learning activities and exchanges.

- In the second Digital Learning Transition MOOC-Ed, 15.5 percent (n = 139) of the participants completed the final survey. They reported, on average, spending 3–4 hours per unit. Survey results show that the large majority of participants report that they made good progress on their personal goals, developed new insights and knowledge, and found the course engaging, motivating, and worth recommending to colleagues.

- With the exception of two experimental synchronous twitter chats, the majority of participants completing the survey found all the elements of the course (e.g., video resource, group discussions, expert panels, projects, etc.) to be valuable. Open-ended comments made it clear that which resources and activities were most valuable varied across participants, confirming the need to provide varied learning options and paths within MOOC-Eds to support the self-directed learning design principle.

- Many participants report that the exchanges with like-minded educators; feedback from colleagues about their goals, challenges, strategies and action steps statements; and information about digital learning transitions from the case studies and expert panel discussions were very useful parts of the course. This confirms the importance of the peer-supported learning and case-study/project-based learning design principles.

- Several types of preliminary discourse analyses show that participants were engaged in reflection, information sharing, and co-construction of ideas in the discussions. While a substantial number of participants contributed to the discussion, we continue to explore ways to increase engagement and interactions in future MOOC-Eds.

- Some participants reported that the MOOC-Ed was particularly valuable in the context of their work with local teams, and others reported it was valuable in the context of a North Carolina blended professional development program for principals. This feedback supports integrating MOOC-Eds with other professional learning activities, while the more detailed comments also point to the need for further work on how to make this type of integration work smoothly.

General Results about the DLT MOOC-Eds

We organize this section around some key questions similar to those asked about all MOOCs.

Are Educators Interested in MOOC-Eds as a Vehicle for Their Own Professional Development?

We publicized each of the two DLT MOOC-Eds through press releases and social networking during the two months prior to the start of each course. Given the target audience for the course (K-12 education leaders) and the topic (planning for the digital learning transition) we did not expect the huge numbers that register for other types of MOOCs. We began with a goal of 500 participants and ended up with 2,665 individuals registered for the first DLT MOOC-Ed and 1,791 for the second. These 4,456 registrants included individuals from all 50 States and D.C. and, to our surprise, since we had not made any effort to promote the courses internationally, more than 10 percent (462) were from other countries, with 90 countries represented. Canada, Pakistan, Great Britain, Australia, Brazil, India, and South Africa had the largest representations; and individuals from Nigeria and Kyrgyzstan were among the most active discussion participants. These data and the responses to additional MOOC-Eds confirm that significant interest exists among educators worldwide in exploring this new form of professional learning.

Which Educators are Interested in the DLT MOOC-Eds?

Overall, the DLT MOOC-Eds attracted educators in a variety of roles that comprised the target audience for the design of the course. Given the range of responsibilities, types of schools, levels of experience, and technology fluency, the need for self-directed learning and alternative ways to engage in the MOOC-Ed seems validated.

Table 9.1 shows the primary areas of responsibility of the enrollees across the two DLT MOOC-Eds. As expected, the largest number of participants (28 percent) identified their primary area of responsibility as instructional technology, which reflects the focus of the courses. Teachers, school and district administrators, and staff responsible for curriculum, professional development, and technology infrastructure were also well represented. The 13 percent listed as

TABLE 9.1 Primary areas of responsibility for participants in DLT1 and DLT2

Primary Area of Responsibility	Number	Percentage
Instructional technology	1249	28
Classroom teaching	729	16
School or district administration	709	16
Other education profession	566	13
Curriculum and Instruction	564	13
Professional development	336	8
Technology infrastructure, ops, finance	275	6
Student	28	1

other education professionals included consultants, vendors, University faculty, and staff at non-profit education organizations.

The majority of registrants were from public non-charter schools or districts (66 percent); others were from private schools (15 percent) and from public charter schools (5 percent); while the remaining participants (14 percent) were not employed by a school or district.

The large majority of registrants reported significant experience in K-12 education, with 69 percent in DLT1 reporting more than 10 years of experience and those in DLT2 reporting an average of 15.9 years of experience, with a range of 0 to 48 years. Almost all participants had college degrees; 66 percent listed a master's degree as their highest degree earned and 11 percent reported having doctoral degrees. This is consistent with the roles of the participants and the target audience of those involved in planning and implementing innovative initiatives. The participants were 61 percent female and 39 percent male, which reflects the larger number of females working in K-12 education. Most of those enrolled (86 percent) reported some experience with online learning and 43 percent reported some experience teaching online. Only 25 percent reported prior experience taking a MOOC, but almost all reported that they were experienced in using productivity tools and online networking, so it was a technology-sophisticated group of educators.

Was There Active Participation in the MOOC-Ed?

At a global level, these data show significant activity over the course of each of the two MOOC-Eds: more than 45,000 page views, 5,000 hours on the course site (and many more hours reviewing linked resources external to the site), over 1,800 participants in the discussions posting more than 6,000 messages and more

TABLE 9.2 Participant activity in DLT1 and DLT2

	DLT1	DLT2	Total
Number enrolled	2,665	1,791	4,456
Countries represented	60	60	90
Visits to course site	21,172	24,724	45,896
Page views of course site	96,404	100,834	197,238
Hours on course site			
(excluding external video and text resources)	2,364	2,653	5,017
Discussion participants	962	895	1,857
Number of discussion postings	2,822	3,575	6,397
Number of discussion pages viewed	74,580	42,173	116,753
Views of the videos developed for the course (excluding the many videos from other organizations)	6,028	5,041	11,069

than 116,000 views of those messages, along with more than 11,000 views of the course-specific videos. Certainly, these numbers are far higher than we would find in comparable data from two face-to-face eight-week courses on the same topic.

The table also shows that while DLT2 had 40 percent of the total enrollees for the two courses, it had more page views and discussion postings. This is likely due to some revisions in the course, including the addition of an *introduce yourself* section of the forum that was very active in Unit 1. It may also be that DLT2 had fewer enrollees who were just curious about MOOCs and did not actively participate.

How Many of Those Who Enrolled Actively Participated?

The short answer is that some do, but far fewer than those who enroll; and participation declines significantly over the weeks of the course. The analyses of the decline in participation and other analyses below are from the DLT2 MOOC-Ed data, since we have more detailed analytics available for that course than the prior one.

We began with 1,791 enrollees in DLT2. We removed 46 who were staff in the organizations offering the course or expert panelists for the course, since those were not typical participants. We then classified those who made at least one visit to the unit as an *active participant* in a unit. Just over half (907) met this criterion in Unit 1, so that is the number we count as active participants at the start of the DLT 2 MOOC-Ed. Many of these individuals introduced themselves in the Unit 1 discussion but did not return for Unit 2, which had 503 active participants. Figure 9.3 shows the decline in active participants across the eight units of the course. Clearly, information about enrollee numbers can significantly misrepresent how many people actively participate in a MOOC, even with the very lenient criteria for participation of at least one visit to a unit, so we distinguish between *enrollees* and *participants*.

Note that units were made available on a weekly basis so, for example, Unit 4 was not available until the start of Week 4. Since once a unit is opened it remains open for the rest of the course, participants may be working on units prior to the current one at any time. Our analyses have shown that after the first week of the course as many as 50 percent of the participants spend time on units prior to the most recent one. This, and requests from participants, led us to keep the course open for additional weeks after the original end date. Figure 9.4 below shows the number of participants who visited the course during each week, including two additional weeks after the release of the final unit (P1 and P2) to provide participants with additional time finishing their work in the course.

These data show that many participants did not begin the course until the second week, since there were 907 participants in Unit 1 but only 596 participants during the first week. There is then a decline in participation each week, with participation continuing at a reduced rate into weeks 9 and 10.

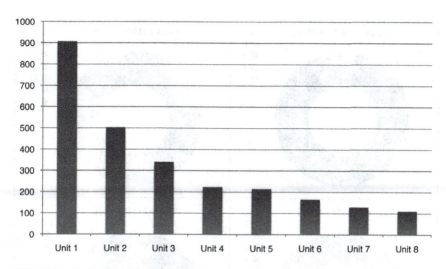

FIGURE 9.3 Active participants by unit

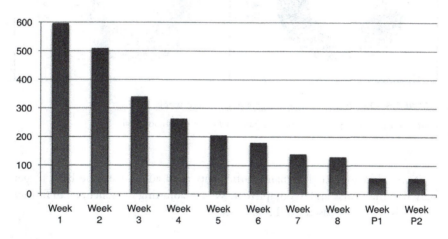

FIGURE 9.4 Number of active participants by week

The circle graphs in Figure 9.5 provide another way to view the pattern of activity across units and weeks during the second half of the course and the two additional weeks (P1 and P2) provided after the planned end of the course. The Week 5 circle shows that during that week, only 50 percent of the page clicks were on the Unit 5 content; the other half were on the prior units. In each of weeks 6, 7, and 8, less than 40 percent of the page clicks were on the schedule units for those weeks. Only by the second post-course week did page clicks in Unit 8 reach 40 percent.

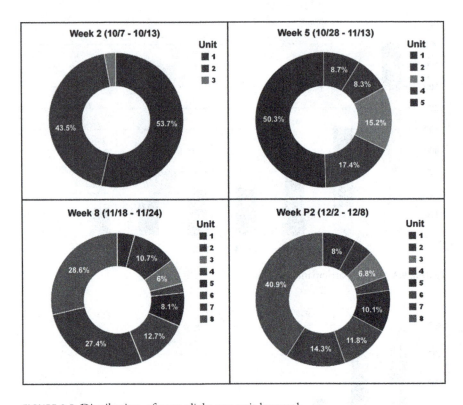

FIGURE 9.5 Distribution of page clicks per unit by week

Source: Image courtesy of the Friday Institute for Educational Innovation.

These data suggest that many participants need additional time both to get started in the course and to complete it. We are adjusting the schedules of further DLT MOOC-Eds based on this analysis.

How Much Time Do Participants Spend on the Course?

Table 9.3 shows the distribution of responses to the question of: *On average, how many hours per units have you spent on MOOC-Ed activities?* A typical DLT2 participant (44 percent) reported spending 3–4 hours per week, with 31 percent reporting less and 25 percent reporting more. The percentages from the DLT1 final survey are very similar.

These results, along with data from other courses, suggest designing for a core group that has three to four hours of engagement per week, while providing options for those who have more or less time available.

TABLE 9.3 Average hours spent on each unit

Hours	Total	% Responding
1–2 hours per unit	42	30.7
3–4 hours per unit	60	43.8
5–6 hours per unit	30	21.9
7–8 hours per unit	4	2.9
More than 8 hours per unit	1	0.7
Total responses	137	100

How Many Participants Completed the Course?

MOOC-Eds differ from college courses in many ways, including that they do not have formal tests, grades, and completion requirements. With our audience of adult professionals who have different goals for taking the course, our measure of success is how many participants are able to advance on their personal goals, not how many meet an instructor-defined criteria for "completion." However, we did have one metric that could be considered completion. Many educators need a certain number of continuing education units (CEUs) within a certain time period. To enable participants to obtain CEUs, we offered certification of 20 hours of professional development to those who requested it and who:

- submitted their statements, individually or as part of a team, of goals, challenges, strategies, and action steps;
- provided constructive reviews of the statements submitted by at least six other participants;
- contributed at least six postings to the discussion forum;
- completed the end-of-course survey;
- certified that they spent at least 20 hours on DLT MOOC-Ed activities.

In DLT2, of the 907 participants who began the course, 67 requested and received certificates of completion of these requirements for CEUs. So by the strictest criteria we can apply, 7.4 percent of the initial active participants completed the course. However, not all participants needed or wanted a certificate of completion and, as shown in Table 9.3 above, there were 111 participants active in the final unit, so by that measure 12.2 percent completed the course. In addition, many participants found the course to be of value to them in meeting their goals, which we consider the more critical definition of success.

Results Related to Self-Directed Learning

To support *self-directed learning*, the DLT MOOC-Ed needs to enable participants with different goals, interests, and learning preferences to choose alternative paths through the course, selecting the resources, discussions, and activities that they would find most beneficial. In this section, we summarize our findings related to this design principle.

What Were the Participants' Goals for Taking the DLT MOOC-Ed?

We collected this information in different ways across the two DLT MOOC-Eds. For the first (DLT1), the registration survey contained an open-ended question asking participants to specify up to three goals for taking the course. We used the results to develop a set of choices for the second DLT MOOC-Ed (DLT2), asking participants to choose up to three of the provided options, while also allowing them to specify other goals.

Table 9.4 shows the number of participants in DLT2 who specified each goal. The four most frequently chosen goals, with more than 30 percent of participants including among their three goals, were: *Prepare to lead change in my school or district* (44.0 percent); *Understand the potential of digital learning* (40.5 percent); *Learn about best practices for DLT transitions* (37.6 percent); and *Plan more effective professional development for local teachers* (30.1 percent). These are consistent with the overall intent of the course. Some of the selected goals, such as *become a better coach or mentor for other teachers* (selected by 20.8 percent of participants) and *improve my own classroom teaching* (selected by 16.0 percent), were not primary goals of the course design, but the course did contain information that participants could use to address these goals.

TABLE 9.4 Goals selected by registrants in DLT2 (each could select up to three)

Goal	Total	Participants (%)
Prepare to lead change in my school or district	792	44.0
Understand the potential of digital learning	728	40.5
Learn about best practices for DLT transitions	676	37.6
Plan more effective professional development for local teachers	541	30.1
Become a better coach or mentor for other teachers	374	20.8
Understand the benefits and risks of technology in K–12 schools	319	17.7
Improve my own classroom teaching	288	16.0
Experience a MOOC	271	15.1
Engage my community in supporting digital learning	266	14.8
Connect with other educators who lead DLT initiatives	262	14.6
Learn about approaches to K–12 infrastructures and devices	248	13.8
Organize and inform the work of our local team	228	12.7
Understand and plan for the financial realities of DLT initiatives	119	6.6
Learn how to create a safe internet environment for students	106	5.9

Did Participants Meet Their Personal Goals and Benefit from Participating in the DLT MOOC-Ed?

Given our principle of self-directed learning, this is an important question. Our best data to address this question comes from the end of course survey. A total of 139 participants completed the survey, 15.5 percent of those who began the course, just over twice the number who requested certificates of completion, and comparable to the number who were active in the last two weeks and units of the course.

Table 9.5 shows the final survey items most relevant to participants' views of the value of the course and their satisfaction with it. They were asked to rate each statement on a scale from 1 (not at all true) to 5 (very true).

Taking responses of 3, 4, or 5 as showing some agreement, these data show that at least 90 percent of the participants reported that they made progress on their personal goals; were engaged in the MOOC-Ed experience; developed new insights and knowledge that would enable them to further digital learning in K-12 education; became more motivated to do so; and would recommend future DLT MOOC-Eds to colleagues. If we consider the 128 participants who agreed that they had made progress on their goals to have "completed" the course, we now have 14 percent of those who participated in Unit 1. Of course, we do not know if others who did not complete the survey would also agree with this statement, so the actual number may be higher.

TABLE 9.5 Satisfaction and value of MOOC-Ed to participants of DLT2

Satisfaction	1 (%)	2 (%)	3 (%)	4 (%)	5 (%)	Avg.	N
I feel like I have made good progress on my personal goals	4.3	3.6	23.7	46.8	21.6	3.8	139
I have been engaged in and am enjoying the MOOC-Ed experience	3.7	5.9	13.2	37.5	39.7	4.0	136
I developed new insights and knowledge that will enable me to better contribute to furthering digital learning in K-12 education	2.2	5.0	9.4	38.1	45.3	4.2	139
I feel motivated to address the need to further digital learning in my school or district	2.2	2.9	12.3	34.1	48.6	4.2	138
I would recommend that my colleagues participate in future Digital Learning Transition MOOCs for Educators	4.4	3.6	10.2	25.5	56.2	4.3	137

In What Ways and to What Extent did Participants Personalize Their Learning (Choose Different Paths through the MOOC-Ed) to Meet Their Learning Goals?

This is an important question in our research, since understanding different pathways that participants take through the MOOC-Ed would help us design courses that enable productive, self-directed learning for more educators. We are just beginning to explore this topic, so offer some preliminary ideas and data here.

Participants did not necessarily participate in a linear way or go through the activities in a particular order. Similarly, participants chose to engage (or not engage) in different elements and resources in the course.

In our final survey, we asked participants to rate the value of each of the elements of the course. The results are shown in Table 9.6. With the exception of two experimental Twitter chats (which we will not necessarily continue in future DLT MOOC-Eds), at least 85 percent of respondents who completed the final survey used each type of activity provided in the course. We will be seeking ways to obtain data from more participants throughout the course in the future.

Combining the ratings of 4 and 5 into a *valuable* response, we find that more than three-quarters found the video resources, text resources, and expert panel videos to be valuable. About two-thirds found the introductory videos (we are working on improving those for future courses), group discussions and projects valuable. Fewer, but still well over half, found the project feedback and the additional suggested resources to be valuable. Data on the same questions midway through the course (Unit 4) provided similar patterns, with 117 respondents.

TABLE 9.6 Value of elements of the course to participants of DLT2

Element	1 (%)	2 (%)	3 (%)	4 (%)	5 (%)	Did Not Use (%)	Avg.	N
Introductory video presentations	3.6	8.7	17.4	38.4	29.0	2.9	3.8	138
Video resources	0.7	6.5	12.3	34.1	44.9	1.4	4.2	138
Text resources	0.7	2.2	15.9	39.9	39.1	2.2	4.2	138
Group discussions	2.2	8.7	21.0	37.7	26.1	4.3	3.8	138
Expert panel videos	2.2	5.1	14.5	42.0	34.1	2.2	4.0	138
Goals and challenges project	2.2	0.7	20.3	27.5	38.4	10.9	4.1	138
Project feedback from participants	0.7	6.6	24.3	32.4	23.5	12.5	3.8	136
Participant suggested resources	2.2	1.4	19.6	37.0	24.6	15.2	3.9	138
Twitter chats	5.8	4.4	9.5	12.4	5.8	62.0	3.2	137

In future analyses, we will be exploring whether groups of participants show different patterns of use of the categories of resources. For example, are there video-focused and text-focused participants? Are there participants who mainly value the expert panels and discussions, which tend to focus on more specific "how tos" than other resources?

We also explored the relationship among three variables across all participants in the course: number of course pages viewed, number of discussion forum pages viewed, and number of postings in the discussion forum. Some participants provide comparatively few postings themselves, but are very active readers of other discussion postings. The most active reader of postings viewed 338 postings but did not post a single comment in the forum. Others have a much higher ratio of postings to viewings of others' posts. Similarly, comparing course page views to forum page views and postings shows that some participants were heavy users of the course resources with little use of the discussion forum, while others were more engaged in the forum and made relatively less use of the course resources.

Participants' comments when asked what they found most beneficial about the DLT MOOC-Ed represent how they chose to focus their time and attention in different ways, on different topics, and in different parts of the MOOC-Ed and how they utilized certain parts of the course. Some comments about what participants found most beneficial follow:

- I learned to differentiate and make professional learning learner-centered. This course helped me know how to support my colleagues.
- The expert panels have all been very helpful in beginning dialogs with other administrative personnel in the district.
- All the video resources were wonderful. I learned a lot from each one. I took from the course the importance of communication to all key stakeholders. Also how vital it is to have a strong team in place to move the transition forward.
- Readings were great. I can download and review at own pace.
- The benefits of seeing/hearing where other educators were on this journey . . . and how they overcame or are overcoming obstacles.
- Being able to articulate my journey. . . . Encouragement and energy coming from the fact that so many educators are in similar places and working toward similar objectives.
- This course has helped me to understand and realize the potential of digital learning in K–12 schools. It provided me great opportunities to communicate and collaborate with others.
- The volume of the resources was overwhelming at times, but I appreciated the opportunity to personalize the learning by choosing the resources that applied to my situation.
- The action plans, goal setting, and strategies have been helpful. They allowed me to put my thoughts together. Expert panels confirmed the thoughts I had about implementing a DLT and also taught me new things.

- I found that the last two units really assisted me with moving forward in my planning and understanding. I think this was because this was the area where I needed more assistance in my own learning.
- I found it engaging and "walking the talk"—one could proceed at their own pace and with their own choices, but were put on track with many resources to assist learning.

Overall, analyses of participants' goals and self-directed learning suggest two lessons for future MOOC-Eds: (1) The need to continue to provide alternative resources, projects, and paths to enable participants to meet their own goals through self-directed, peer-supported learning; and (2) the need to clearly communicate what goals a specific MOOC-Ed is *and is not* intended to meet. For example, the DLT MOOC-Ed is designed for those involved in planning school and district initiatives, but is not intended to address in detail classroom practices in specific content areas and grade levels. Defining and communicating the purposes of a MOOC-Ed so that potential participants can determine whether it fits their goals and interests is an important consideration for the success of MOOC-Eds.

Results Related to Peer-Supported Learning

Peer-supported learning takes place in the DLT MOOC-Ed through (1) the discussion forum in each course, (2) the crowdsourcing about valuable resources and ideas, and (3) the peer feedback to the two sections of the project—the first on goals and challenges and the second that adds strategies and action steps.

Open-ended responses show that these elements were highly valued by some participants:

- The greatest benefit that MOOC-Ed has granted to me was the contact with like-minded educators.
- The MOOC provided a structured environment for me to create an initiative with support from educators around the world. I was energized both by the content I viewed/read and the discussions with other participants. I felt like other participants were very engaged and offered realistic, thoughtful feedback. The crowdsourcing of the resources helped me focus on the most important resources for sharing with others.
- The best part was suggestions/ideas/feedback/participation in online discussions. These helped me in framing an action plan for my own professional development and design an action plan to help the coordinators working under me.
- Feedback from colleagues was the most beneficial part. Also, it helped to know that so many of us are in similar situations and have similar challenges and experiences.

- The discussion forum was most reflective and helpful as I learned about the barriers and its solutions to promote digital learning in my schools.
- I loved seeing others from all different locations talking about the same thing—passion for the students, for the schools, and for digital learning. The interaction with others was so great—Everyone has such great ideas and opinions and to pool them all together like this was amazing. Well done!
- Just received all the "tools" (Chromebooks, bags, charging carts) this week at our school to begin a 1:1 program. Although I am as excited as a kid at Christmas, I have stayed awake many nights lately stressing about starting the program. However, the discussion and the many insightful comments that I have read have given me some confidence to dive in and start the transformation at my school.

We designed the course so that there are specifically focused discussions embedded into each unit, while the entire discussion forum could also be accessed separately. We begin in the first two units by dividing participants into smaller groups according to the first letter of their state or country, in order to keep the number of people in a discussion manageable while keeping those from the same places together. In Units 3 and 4, participants are then grouped for discussion according to whether they are working on a plan for a classroom, school, district, or other educational organization. In later units, discussions focus on specific topics (e.g., technology infrastructure, assessment, community connections) so that participants can select those of interest to them. The comments are not threaded, so are all at the same level and organized by time of posting. Options to quote prior postings and to mark postings as "agree," "disagree," or "insightful" are available, and those that receive at least five positive ratings are flagged for other participants. The course facilitators seeded initial discussion topics and added comments to maintain some presence in the course and move the discussions along, but most of the discussions were initiated and driven by the participants.

As noted above, different participants made different levels of use of the discussion forum, and the ratio of discussion postings to views varies widely across participants. Survey responses from participants, also described above, show that about 67 percent of respondents rated the group discussion to be valuable and well over 50 percent found the feedback about projects and peer-suggested resources to be valuable.

What Types of Exchanges Took Place in the Online Discussions?

The discussion forums also provide a rich set of exchanges that can be analyzed in many different ways. In a related MOOC Research Initiative project, Shaun Kellogg, Sherry Booth, and Kevin Oliver (2014) at the Friday Institute have begun with two types of discourse analyses, which are described below. They are also applying social network analysis techniques, which will be reported separately. Updated research reports will be available at www.mooc-ed.org. A summary of their analyses to date is provided below.

We analyzed the content of the discussions in two ways. The first looks at the five discourse characteristics of the postings adapted from the Transcript Analysis Tool (Fahy, Crawford, & Ally, 2001):

1. Statements. Convey facts, information, or direct answers/comments to preceding posts.
2. Scaffolding. Initiate, continue, or acknowledge interpersonal interactions.
3. References. Quote or directly refer to other sources.
4. Reflections. Express the individual's thoughts, judgments, or opinions in a way that welcomes responses.
5. Questions. Invite others to provide answers or information.

Figure 9.6 shows the results from a stratified sample of the discussions. (The initial *introduce yourself* discussion was not included, since it was intended to have primarily statements.)

The data show that, other than statements, scaffolding was the most common characteristic among postings, followed by references, reflections, and questions.

We also applied the Interaction Analysis Model (Gunawardena, Lowe, & Anderson, 1997) to assess the extent to which the interactions among educators resulted in the co-construction of knowledge. This analysis classifies each discussion into one of the following five phases according to the highest phase reached in the postings under that discussion:

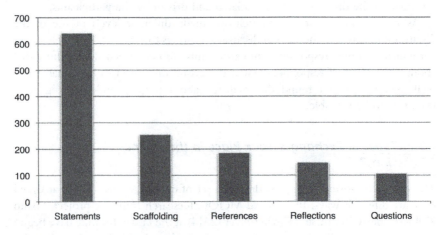

FIGURE 9.6 Discourse characteristics of postings

1. Sharing and comparing. Further the discussion by providing observations, opinions, or examples that support or extend prior statements.
2. Dissonance and inconsistency. Identify areas of disagreement or potential disagreement.
3. Negotiation and co-construction. Explore common ground, clarify intent, seek agreement, or integrate ideas.
4. Testing and modification. Test ideas against prior information, research and/or data, and proposed synthesis of ideas.
5. Summary, application, and metacognition. Summarize agreements, describe applications of knowledge, or acknowledge changes in understanding.

The data, shown in Figure 9.7, display the proportions of discussions by the highest phase of knowledge construction reached in a discussion thread.

The data show that nearly half the discussions reach the negotiation and co-construction level, which suggests productive exchanges are taking place. It is also interesting to note that this analysis shows far more postings at level 3, negotiation and co-construction, than at level 2, dissonance and inconsistency. That is consistent with two observations of the discussions: (1) the participating educators very rarely directly expressed disagreement and (2) of the three tags participants could select for every posting, those of agree and insightful were used often, while disagree was almost never used. Participants seem very hesitant to directly express disagreement with each other.

These analyses suggest that DLT MOOC-Eds are fairly successful in stimulating engaged and productive interactions, which is consistent with the view of

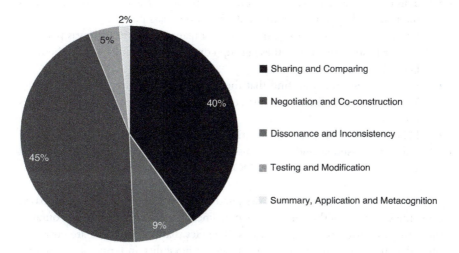

FIGURE 9.7 Highest phase of knowledge construction reached at the discussion level

those who followed the discussions—we've been impressed by the number of thoughtful postings and lengthy exchanges.

Results Related to Integration into Blended Learning Programs

We believe that MOOC-Eds can provide valuable professional learning experiences for many educators, but that they become most valuable when combined with other face-to-face or online learning opportunities. For example, the DLT MOOC-Ed addresses planning for a K-12 digital learning transition in schools and districts. In practice, this requires a team that brings together expertise in curriculum, assessment, professional development, technology, funding, policy, administration, and communications. The DLT MOOC-Ed includes a large amount of content across these areas and was designed to be most beneficial when groups worked through the course content in teams that were responsible for local planning. When that was not possible, we encouraged participants to work with local colleagues who were also interested in the course. At the time they completed the DLT2 registration survey, the majority of participants, 55 percent, planned to participate with colleagues; 35 percent with a school or district planning team; and 20 percent with other colleagues in their school or organization.

Feedback from participants verified the value of a team approach. Representative comments include:

- The most beneficial aspect of this course was actually the face-to-face conversations informed and occasioned by the MOOC with the other members of my school team.
- This course helped members of our DLT team see the possibilities and open their minds beyond the traditional 45-minute class periods.
- I am happy that we took part as a school team, which in turn was part of a greater District team. It is these group conversations that I found to be most helpful.
- Love the resources and find that there are many to share. We are working as a team in the district on this course and the time we spend together is invaluable.
- [The most valuable part was] meeting as a team at my school weekly to create our self-assessment and the discussions we have had around our goals and what we are learning in the MOOC-Ed.

In addition, the MOOC-Ed is designed to support blended approaches based upon the versatility of the content, the non-linear possibilities, and the encouragement to participate in groups or teams. The fact that MOOC-Eds are currently offered at no cost to participants also provides flexibility in terms of integrating the MOOC-Ed into other initiatives, assuming that the timing works. We have explored using the DLT MOOC-Ed as part of a graduate course, in which students also had their own Google Community site, interactions prior to the MOOC-Ed, and projects after the MOOC-Ed to complete their course requirements. We are also integrating the DLT MOOC-Ed into a yearlong professional development program for North Carolina principals, which involves face-to-face sessions, online modules, and executive coaching components. We are currently exploring other possibilities for wrapping other activities around MOOC-Eds and integrating MOOC-Eds into larger professional learning programs.

Results Related to Case Study and Project Based Learning

Case studies and project based learning are incorporated in the DLT MOOC-Ed through the following:

- school and district case studies in units 2 and 3;
- expert panels, which focused on lessons learned from local initiatives and often included leaders from the case study schools;
- the project that participants were invited to submit that summarized their recommended goals and challenges (Unit 3) and their strategies and action steps (Unit 7) for their local initiative; and
- the peer feedback participants were asked to provide in response to the submitted projects.

A number of participants cited these elements as most valuable in their comments about the course:

- I have learned how other districts and schools have been implementing digital learning. . . . I was able to see a bigger picture than what I am faced with in my daily role in my district and I have enjoyed that.
- I have a great deal more background knowledge about development of digital learning in a K-12 setting. I really appreciate the resources that have been presented and the expert panels have all been very helpful in beginning dialogs with other administrative personnel in the district.
- I particularly benefited from the case study presentations, which gave lots of insight into the successes and challenges of districts that are ahead of our implementation schedule.
- Creating the plan after seeing how others had done it was a great inspiration.
- I felt that the practical ideas and tips from those working in the field were very helpful in understanding how to implement technology and address the challenges that we face.
- I learned that my struggles with technology integration are not unique and it was very beneficial to hear from those who have found solutions to these

problems and are now very successful. I particularly like the expert panel discussions because I would print out the questions posed to the panelists and then take notes on their responses for future reference.

- The Action plans, goal setting, and strategies have been helpful. They allowed me to put my thoughts together. Expert panels confirmed the thoughts I had about implementing a DLT and also taught me new things.
- The goals and challenges statement was very beneficial. It made my team focus on these aspects. Although we knew our challenges, it was more clear once it was formulated on paper.
- I have benefited most from the MOOC-Ed from working with my local team, expert panels, and other resources on the course. Working on our district assessment and goals as well as the discussions we have about the units have helped us stay focused on the big picture of using technology to change the way we teach.

We divided the projects into those that addressed digital learning initiative planning within a classroom, school, district, or other educational organization. We handled peer feedback differently than most other MOOCs. We asked participants to submit their projects as discussions in a designated area of the forum and then to provide constructive feedback to each other as comments. We asked for feedback from at least three participants for each project submission, and participants could choose which ones they would address. This meant that feedback was not anonymous, as it is in many MOOCs, and that participants could read as many projects and comments as they wanted and engage in discussions about the projects and feedback. This is consistent with the belief that MOOC-Eds are about learning, not grades, and that open peer discussions are an important element.

The project was divided into two parts, with goals and challenges submitted in Unit 3 and strategies and action steps added in Unit 7. The number of project statements submitted and the number of comments, by category of project, are shown in Table 9.7. Participants were invited to submit projects as a team, so some of the projects represent the work of multiple participants.

TABLE 9.7 Project statements and comments submitted by category

Category	Part 1 statements submitted	Part 1 feedback comments	Part 2 statements submitted	Part 2 feedback comments
Classroom	14	96	7	44
School	37	152	25	109
District	24	114	10	48
Other organization	30	105	10	45
Total	105	467	52	246

Conclusions

This report is based upon early work on MOOC-Eds, both on the design and development and on the research sides. It does yield some initial insights into our design principles and how we can better instantiate them in the MOOC-Eds. For example, the results suggest the need to provide additional guidance about alternative paths for self-directed learning. The results also confirm the need to provide alternative resources (e.g., a variety of case studies so participants can select those that are similar to their own contexts) and alternative media (e.g., video, podcast and transcript) to fit different participants' needs and preferences.

Our early research leads to a wide range of questions for future research. A few examples include:

- How can participants best be placed in groups to foster productive discussions? What is the optimal size for discussion groups?
- How can discussions be initiated, facilitated, and connected to resources and activities in order to encourage high levels of engagement and exchanges that involve reflection and co-construction?
- How can we best balance having participants move through the units on a common schedule so they can engage in peer-supported learning with providing flexible scheduling to meet educators' needs?
- Can we identify characteristics of participants and preferred self-directed paths through the MOOC-Ed? How can we design future MOOC-Eds to optimize them for participants with different profiles?
- What types of case studies and projects are most engaging and beneficial for participants? What guidance and structures lead to productive peer feedback?
- Can participation be further incentivized by the use of badges or other forms of recognition?
- What impact do MOOC-Eds have on professional knowledge, skills, and practices?
- How can MOOC-Eds best be integrated with other professional development activities?

Our experience developing, offering, and researching MOOC-Eds, both what has been reported in this chapter and other related work, strongly confirms our initial hypotheses that this approach to professional learning is a valuable addition that can help address the needs of the K-12 education workforce. We continue to believe that MOOCs are best suited to adult, motivated professionals, and that our work and research on other types of MOOCs supports that view. We find that our design principles of self-directed learning, peer-supported learning, case study and project-based learning, and blended learning have merit as a foundation for MOOC-Eds, but that there are many complex design decisions involved in making an individual course of value to a large and diverse audience of educators. We are especially interested in the roles MOOCs can play as part of pre-service preparation and ongoing professional learning for educators, since they can provide valuable learning opportunities but do not replace local professional learning teams, coaching, peer collaborations, or face-to-face programs. The important question, we believe, is not *Do MOOC-Eds work?* but rather *How can we optimize the value of MOOC-Eds?*, *What professional learning needs can best be addressed by MOOC-Eds?*, and *How are MOOC-Eds best blended with other professional learning activities to support educators in providing the education our children need to be prepared for college, careers, and citizenship in the digital information age?* We look forward to continuing our work in addressing those questions.

Note

1   The authors thank Blythe Tyrone, Mark Samberg, John Bass, and Ryan Kilby for their important contributions to developing and running the Digital Learning Transition MOOC-Eds; Mark Samberg, Isaac Thompson, Shaun Kellogg, Sherry Booth, and Kevin Oliver for their valuable contributions to the data analyses reported in this chapter; and all the DLT MOOC-Ed participants from whom we have learned so much.

References

Booth, S., Kellogg, S., & Oliver, K. (2014). A social network perspective on peer supported learning in MOOCs for educators. *The International Review of Research in Open and Distance Learning*. Manuscript submitted for publication.

Darling-Hammond, L., Wei, R., Andree, A., Richardson, N., & Orphanos, S. (2009). *Professional learning in the learning profession: A status report on teacher development in the United States and abroad*. Dallas, TX: National Staff Development Council.

Fahy, P. J., Crawford, G., & Ally, M. (2001). Patterns of interaction in a computer conference transcript. *International Review of Research in Open and Distance Learning*, 2(1).

Gunawardena, C. N., Lowe, C. A., & Anderson, T. (1997). Analysis of a global online debate and the development of an interaction analysis model for examining social construction of knowledge in computer conferencing. *Journal of Educational Computing Research*, 17(4), 395–429.

iNACOL (2011). *National standards for quality online teaching*. Vienna, VA: iNACOL. www.k12hsn.org/files/research/Online_Learning/iNACOL_TeachingStandardsv2.pdf

National Center for Education Statistics (2014). *Digest of Education Statistics: 2012*. http://nces.ed.gov/programs/digest/d12/index.asp

Wei, R. C., Darling-Hammond, L., & Adamson, F. (2010). *Professional development in the United States: Trends and challenges*. Dallas, TX. National Staff Development Council.

CONTRIBUTING AUTHORS

Samantha Adams Becker, Senior Director of Communications for the New Media Consortium, is the lead writer and researcher for the NMC Horizon Report series, which analyzes emerging technology uptake in various education sectors across the globe. She has an expertise in digital communications and community-building, with a special interest in e-publishing and social media. Samantha manages the NMC's communication efforts through more than 15 content platforms. Previous to the NMC, she facilitated the digitization of books and periodicals for several of the world's largest publishers, including HarperCollins and Harlequin, and was the Managing Editor of a lifestyle and arts-focused magazine.

Dr. Sian Bayne is Professor of Digital Education in the School of Education at the University of Edinburgh. She convenes the Digital Cultures and Education research group, and is Associate Dean (digital scholarship) in the College of Humanities and Social Science. She teaches on the MSc in Digital Education and the E-learning and Digital Cultures MOOC. Her research interests revolve around educational change as we become more and more enmeshed with the digital. Current particular interests are around posthumanism and online education, the geographies of distance education, open education, and multimodal academic literacies.
Twitter: @sbayne
Web: sianbayne.net

Samantha Bernstein is a licensed attorney and Ph.D. student of urban education policy at the University of Southern California's Rossier School of Education. Her research interests include technology and intellectual property, openness in the university setting, and the future of the academic profession. She is currently working with Dr. Adrianna Kezar on issues relating to organizational change in higher education.

Meg Evans leads Udemy for Good, the social impact arm of Udemy, a global online marketplace for teaching and learning. In this role, she is working to democratize education by partnering with international organizations and non-profits to help local content experts abroad share their expertise with the world. Previously she worked with the Clayton Christensen Institute for Disruptive Innovation where she wrote on blended learning as a necessary strategy for reform and policy challenges surrounding innovation.

Dr. David Frye is the Associate Director of The Friday Institute for Educational Innovation, an institute at the NC State University College of Education that fosters collaborations to advance education through innovation in teaching, learning, and leadership. An education administrator and strategic leader by background, Dave has led innovative programs and initiated new uses for technology to develop college students into future campus and community leaders in the Midwest and Southeast. As a member of the team that founded The Friday Institute, Dave works with leading researchers, educators, and policy-makers to create a unique, collaborative environment and identify strategic initiatives for developing real-world, research-based solutions to education's grand challenges.

Professor Jeff Haywood (BSc, PhD, FRSA) is Vice-Principal Knowledge Management, CIO, and Librarian at the University of Edinburgh. He is head of the University's integrated Information Service, offering a wide range of services in Library, IT, Technology-Enhanced Learning, and Classroom Technology. Jeff leads many major University-wide initiatives, including the substantial expansion of taught online distance Masters degrees, and Massive Open Online Courses (MOOCs).

As Professor of Education & Technology in the University's School of Education, his research interests are in the development of strategies for effective use of ICT in education at institutional, national, and international levels.

Jeff is a past member of the JISC Board, past Chair of the eLearning Task Force for the Coimbra Group, and a current member of the Scottish Government's ICT for Excellence Group, designing the next generation digital learning environment for Scottish schools.

Victor Hu is the Global Head of Education Technology & Services investment banking at Goldman, Sachs & Co., which advises, finances, and invests in leading education companies around the world. Victor holds an MBA from the Wharton School of the University of Pennsylvania, a JD from Harvard Law School, and a Bachelors of Arts from Amherst College. Victor is originally from Taipei, Taiwan and currently lives in San Francisco with his wife and two daughters. The views expressed in this article are personal and do not represent views of Goldman Sachs.

Dr. Larry Johnson serves as Chief Executive Officer of the New Media Consortium, an international not-for-profit consortium dedicated to the exploration and use of new media and new technologies. Its hundreds of member institutions constitute an elite list of the most highly regarded universities, museums, and research centers in the world. The NMC's dozen-year exploration of technology use in education, the Horizon Project, informs strategic technology planning for educational institutions in more than 175 countries. As the project's founder, Johnson works with visionaries and thought leaders from across the globe to define new ways of thinking about technology, and explore emerging trends and issues.

Dr. Paul Kim is the Chief Technology Officer and Assistant Dean at the Stanford University Graduate School of Education. Dr. Kim has been leading numerous projects involving the design of learning technologies, educational research, and international development. He is a senior researcher for the Programmable Open Mobile Internet (POMI) project (http://pomi.stanford.edu/) in which he designs and experiments future mobile technologies and global classroom solutions. He implemented various mobile learning pedagogies such as SMILE (Stanford Mobile Inquiry-based Learning Environment) in over 22 countries while launching a MOOC on Venture Lab (http://venture-lab.org/education/), attracting over 20,000 students from around the world.

Dr. Glenn M. Kleiman is the Executive Director of the Friday Institute for Educational Innovation and a Professor at the NC State University College of Education. A cognitive psychologist by background (Ph.D., Stanford, 1977), his work in education has spanned basic and applied research, curriculum development, software development, providing professional development for teachers and administrators, policy analyses, and consulting for school districts and state departments of education. Prior to joining NC State University in July 2007, he was Vice President and Senior Research Scientist at Education Development Center, Inc. (EDC) in Newton MA, where he directed the Center for Online Professional Education and was Co-Director of the Northeast and Islands Regional Education Lab. He was also on the faculty of the Harvard Graduate School of Education from 1995–2007 and was Education Chair of the Harvard/EDC Leadership and the New Technologies Institutes. Dr. Kleiman was a member of the North Carolina eLearning Commission and played a lead role in the development of the North Carolina Race to the Top proposal, which received $400 million of funding from the U.S. Department of Education. Currently, Dr. Kleiman leads The Friday Institute's Massive Online Open Courses for Educators (MOOC-Ed) initiative and directs the development of North Carolina's statewide digital learning plan.

Dr. Jane E. Klobas is a Fellow of the Arts, Science and Knowledge and Dondena Research Centres at Bocconi University, Italy and Adjunct Professor in the School of Engineering and Information Technology at Murdoch University, Australia. She has taught distance, open, online, blended, and classroom-based courses, and has been director of local and international postgraduate courses, including a Masters degree in online education and training. She regularly addresses international conferences on e-learning. Her research is published in books and journals such as *Computers in Human Behavior*, *Internet Research*, and *Educational Technology and Society*.

Dr. Bruce Mackintosh is an Adjunct Associate Professor and Honorary Research Fellow at the University of Western Australia (UWA), and an independent consultant in international education. He has had extensive experience in this field, principally as Director of the International Centre at UWA and briefly as Head of the International Office of the University of Westminster, London. He has attended and presented at numerous international conferences. He is a past Chair of the Australian Universities International Directors' Forum and Deputy Chair of Perth Education City.

Dr. Hamish Macleod has a background in psychology and biology, and is now a Senior Lecturer in the School of Education at the University of Edinburgh in Scotland, having taught for many years in the University's Department of Psychology. He has also spent time as a member of the University's Centre for Teaching, Learning & Assessment (the institution's educational development unit), but is now primarily involved teaching on the University's MSc in Digital Education (http://online.education.ed.ac.uk/). He has long standing interests in the uses of information technology, particularly computer-mediated communications, social technologies, and digital games and simulations, in teaching and learning. Currently he is one of the team behind the E-Learning and Digital Cultures MOOC offered by Edinburgh in partnership with Coursera (www.coursera.org/course/edc).

Dr. Jamie Murphy is the Research Director at the Australian School of Management. His background includes European Marketing Manager for PowerBar and Greg Lemond Bicycles, Lead Academic for the Google Online Marketing Challenge, and a Ph.D. from Florida State University. Dr. Murphy's industry and academic experience spans continents and includes hundreds of academic publications and presentations, as well as dozens of *New York Times* and *Wall Street Journal* stories. His research focus is on the effective use of the Internet for citizens, businesses, and governments, particularly MOOCs.

Farnaz Ronaghi is co-founder and director of engineering at NovoEd. She is also a Ph.D. candidate in the department of Management Science and Engineering at Stanford University. Ronaghi's thesis on the social incentives in online learning involved the creation of the learning environment that became NovoEd.

Dr. Jen Ross is Lecturer in Digital Education in the School of Education at the University of Edinburgh, and the programme director of the MSc in Digital Education. She is one of the team behind the E-learning and Digital Cultures MOOC. She is active in public engagement work in the area of online and distance learning, currently as a Beltane Parliament Engagement Fellow at the Scottish Parliament. Her research and consultancy focuses on areas including distance education, MOOCs, online writing and reflective practices, digital futures for learning, and digital learning for cultural heritage.
Twitter: @jar
Web: jenrossity.net

Amin Saberi is CEO and co-founder of NovoEd. He is also Associate Professor and 3COM faculty scholar in the Management Science and Engineering Department at Stanford University. His research focuses on algorithms, algorithms and games, and more broadly the intersection of computer and social sciences. He is Co-Director of Social Algorithms Lab, Sloan Fellow, and recipient of the NSF Career Award as well as several best paper awards.

Anne Trumbore (anne@novoed.com) is the Senior Course Designer at NovoEd. Beginning at Coursera in 2012, she has designed dozens of MOOCs and other online classes with an emphasis on collaboration and community. She began designing, and teaching in, online environments at Stanford in 2004 where she taught writing, literature, and grammar at the Online High School and EPGY.

Dr. Mary Ann Wolf is the Director of Digital Learning Programs for the Friday Institute for Educational Innovation at NC State University. Mary Ann has worked closely with federal, state, and local education leaders; policy-makers; and organizations on connecting policy and practice for innovative education reform, digital learning, and instructional practices. Mary Ann played a lead role in developing and facilitating the Digital Learning Transition MOOC-Ed and in establishing the Friday Institute's growing initiative on MOOCs for Educators. She is also a part of the development and facilitation team for the Distinguished Leadership in Practice–Digital Learning for principals across the state in conjunction with NCPAPA. Mary Ann wrote *Innovate to Educate: Education System [Re]Design for Personalized Learning*, an influential report based upon a Symposium held by SIIA, ASCD, and CCSSO. She also co-authored *Culture Shift: Teaching in a Learner-Centered Environment Powered by Digital Learning* for the Alliance for Excellent Education and two reports on "Mobile Learning in North America" for UNESCO and CoSN. Previously, Mary Ann was the Executive Director of the State Educational Technology Directors Association (SETDA). In this position, she worked with education leaders and policymakers in all 50 states to share data and models of how to improve education to ensure America's and our students' competitiveness in the global economy. Mary Ann served on the

Congress on the Future of Content Task Force and was a member of the NAEP Technology Literacy Assessment steering committee. She testified before the US House of Representatives Education and Labor Committee; and SETDA hosted, with the National Science Foundation, *Future of Learning* educational technology showcases for members of Congress and staffers in the House and the Senate.

Dennis Yang is the Chief Executive Officer of San Francisco-based Udemy, a global online learning and teaching marketplace. Since Dennis joined the company, Udemy's student base and revenues have grown by 300 percent annually. Prior to joining Udemy, Mr. Yang was the Senior Vice President of Operations at 4INFO, a leading mobile advertising company. Mr. Yang oversaw all the business operations, as well as the strategic initiatives and corporate partnerships at 4INFO. Mr. Yang has over 15 years of mobile and software solution experience in both consumer and enterprise technology markets. Previously, Mr. Yang captained the Corporate Data Access business at Motorola's Good Technology Group. Earlier in his career, he worked as a venture capitalist and spent time as a management consultant with PWC. Mr. Yang holds an MBA from the Stanford Graduate School of Business and a Bachelor of Science from Northwestern University.

INDEX

accountability 97–98
accreditation 11–12, 28, 33, 111
Adams Becker, S. 61–77
adaptive learning 42, 79, 81
adoption and acceptance 12, 14–15, 18
agile governance 53–54
analytics 8, 27, 38, 41, 57, 104, 113, 125–126
anti-MOOCs 62, 69–71
assessment 11–12, 18, 26, 36, 40, 62, 71, 83, 122; open 4; peer 38, 42
asynchronous learning 4, 6, 18
auditing 15–16, 26
Audsley, S. 28
autonomy 98–99, 112

Bass, S. A. 69
Bayh-Dole Act (1980) 111
Bayne, S. 23–45
behaviorism 25
Bernstein, S. 106–116
big data 71
Blackboard Collaborate 33–34
blended learning 18–19, 103, 120, 126, 142
Booth, S. 139
Brabon, B. 33–34
business models 111; sustainable 78–88

Carr, L. 36–39
celebrity academics 27, 34–35, 39, 41, 52
Chaloux, B. 68
Clow, D. 26
cMOOCs 9, 24–28, 33–34, 40, 42, 107, 113
collaboration 58, 73, 87, 96–99, 101–103, 119; CSCL 3; pedagogy 24–25, 31, 33, 35, 40
completion rates 16, 26, 54, 66, 84, 92, 101; see also engagement patterns
connectivism 3–4, 7, 26, 35, 41, 61–62, 70
constructionism 34, 40–41
constructivism 35, 37
content-focused approach 24, 29–30
continuing education units (CEUs) 133
copyright see intellectual property (IP)
cost/benefit analysis 55–57
Coursera 8, 46–48, 50, 52, 54–56, 61–64, 68; business models 79, 83–84, 86–87; intellectual property 108–109, 112–113; pedagogy 25, 27–28, 31, 40–42
CourseSites 34–35
Creative Commons 109
criticism of MOOCs 61–71
Cuban, L. 69

curriculum design 53
curriculum standards 117

decision making 47, 50, 54
demographics 17, 125
discussion boards 8, 16, 72, 125–126,
    137–139, 141; pedagogy 29, 31, 33,
    35, 37
diversity 14, 26, 36, 91, 118
Downes, S. 4, 9, 12, 24, 61–62

ecosystem model 81
educational theory 1, 64
edX 25, 42, 50, 52, 61–65, 68, 83–84,
    87, 108
Eesley, C. 96, 101–102
email 26, 34–35, 100
engagement patterns 40, 93, 97–102,
    113, 126; see also completion
    rates
entrepreneurship 79, 101
Evans, M. 90–95

faculty interest 51–53
fair use 110
Feldstein, M. 28
Fernando, K. 28
flipped classrooms 4, 18, 25
for-profit companies 79
Franz, P. 28
freemium model 81
Friday Institute 118, 139
Friedman, T. 91
Frye, D. 117–146
FutureLearn 35–41, 48–50, 52, 55

Galil, Z. 67
Google 63–64, 85, 125
Grover, S. 28
Guthrie, D. 66, 71

Hartle, T. W. 68
Haywood, J. 46–60
Head, K. 15
Hennessy, J. 64
hierarchies 15, 39
higher-order engagement 101–102,
    104
Hill, P. 26

Hu, V. 78–89
hybrid MOOCs 25, 33, 69

individual purchase model 80
innovation 3, 18–19, 55, 79, 129
institutional cohesion 50
institutional license model 80
instructivism 33, 35–36, 40
intellectual property (IP) 11, 51,
    106–116

Johnson, L. 61–77

K-12 teachers 117–122, 129, 141,
    145; professional development
    119
Kellogg, S. 139
Kizilcec, R. F. 16, 26
Kleiman, G. M. 117–146
Klobas, J. E. 1–22
Koller, D. 108, 113
Kotter, J. 54

learning managment systems (LMS) 3,
    87
learning objectives 10, 92, 134–135
Lewin, T. 66–67
Liang, F. 68–69
licensing content 110–111
lifelong learning 54, 81, 103
Littlejohn, A. 26

McArthur, J. 41
Mackintosh, B. 1–22
Mackness, J. 26, 28
Macleod, H. 46–60
Mak, S. 26
Margaryan, A. 26
marketplace model 92
Maxon, B. 28
mediated learning spaces 23, 104
Milligan, C. 26
monetization 47, 81–83
MOOC-Eds 117–119, 128–129,
    145–146; blended learning 142;
    design principles 120; Digital
    Learning Transition 121–127;
    discussion boards 141; participation
    patterns 129–133; peer-supported

learning 138–139; personal goals
134–137; project-based learning
143–144
motivation 92–93
multimedia 11
Murphy, J. 1–22

Nelson, C. 112
network effects 82
Ng, A. 108–109
Northedge, A. 41
Norvig, P. 64, 107
NovoEd 96–105

Oliver, K. 139
online distance learning (ODL) 6, 80,
82
open licensing 106–109
open source platforms 8–9, 63, 65, 73,
87
Open University 35, 37, 107
Open2Study 9, 12
openness 4–5, 62, 82, 106–116
operational capacities 46
outcome agreements 57

participation patterns 15–18, 24–27,
30–31, 35, 129–133, 137
Pea, R. 28
pedagogy 3, 7, 10, 15, 18–19, 23–28,
52, 79, 113; AI planning 29–32;
anti-MOOCs 61–63, 66, 69–70;
decision making 40–42, 48;
Futurelearn 35–39; pedagogical
decisions 10–11; of the undead 3
3–35
peer learning 98–99, 119–120, 138–139,
145
peer review 56, 97, 100, 102, 120
Pertriglieri, G. 90
Piech, C. 16, 26
plagiarism 15, 79
professional development 119,
126–128
professionalism 23
project-based learning 99–100, 120, 143,
145

quality assurance (QA) 54, 58

recruitment 57, 59
Rees, J. 66
reputation building 37, 56
research and development (R&D) 52,
56
revenue share model 81
risk management 50
Robinson, B. 28
Ronaghi, F. 96–105
Ross, J. 23–45

Saberi, A. 96–105
scalability 4, 82, 119
Schneider, E. 16, 26, 28
Second Life 30–31
Seelig, T. 100
self-directed learning 27–28, 120, 128,
134, 145
Sharples, M. 36–38
Siemens, G. 4, 12, 24, 61–62, 66, 70, 107
Signature Track 64, 84, 86
situated teaching practices 29
skillsets 91–92
Small Private Online Courses (SPOCs)
14, 35, 103
social interaction 32, 107
social learning 96–105
social networking 3, 18, 34, 38, 96,
128–129, 140
sponsorship model 81
Stewart, B. 26
story-telling 37
student loans 63
student-created content 9, 97
surveys 113, 123, 125–127, 132–136,
139, 142

Tapson, J. 66
Tate, A. 29–30, 32
teacher performance 35
teacher roles 27, 29, 33–34, 41–42
teacher visibility 32, 38, 41
teaching culture 41
teamwork 98–99
Thrun, S. 64–66, 85–86, 107–108
Trumbore, A. 96–105

Udacity 8, 62–66, 68, 71, 79, 83, 85–86,
108–109

Udemy 92–94
UK 29, 33, 35–36, 42, 50, 107
unique selling proposition (USP) 59
USA 17, 36, 48, 50, 78–80, 126
utilitarianism 17–18

Varney, K. 28
venture capital 78–79, 88

Watters, A. 62
Wessel, M. 111

Wickler, G. 29
Williams, R. 26
Wolf, M. A. 117–146

xMOOCs 7–11, 15, 24–25, 27, 29–34,
36, 40, 107–109, 113

Yang, D. 90–95
YouTube 50, 63